Sinners
Anonymous

Sinners Anonymous

H. S. Vigeveno

WORD BOOKS, Publishers
Waco, Texas—London, England

Sinners Anonymous

Library of Congress Catalog Card No.: 74–91947

Printed in the United States of America

Contents

How To Right the Wrong

Sinners Anonymous

"If I were not convinced that Christ is risen and that he lives . . . I probably could not have drawn any other conclusion except that of leaving the church. . . . Only the friends I have in it, those who bravely endure to persevere in a life of devotion and sacrifice, would make it hard for me to leave. And what binds me to them most of all is precisely this, that they suffer because of the church just as I do."

—HELMUT THIELICKE[1]

"The chief trouble with the Church is that you and I are in it."

—CHARLES HEIMSATH

I.

An Introduction: Why?

FINDING things wrong with Christians is as easy as jumping on sand castles at the beach. And destroying sand castles as well as spotting hypocrites in the Church has always been a popular pastime in America. Not that the art of judging is reserved for Americans; people everywhere do it. The fact is that Americans on the whole tend to be quite lenient.

There's really no problem playing the critic, for, of course, it's always easier to smash sand castles than to build them. With this difference—sand castles are built on sand; the Church is built on a rock. And although the Church has been attacked, ridiculed and ignored, the foundation remains firm and the structure has often been rebuilt.

I do not wish to write a defense of the Church. Many such attempts have been made. There is no need to add another. Rather, I'm writing to expose the sickness of the Church, its wounds and its deterioration. Once we operate, there can be healing. I'm writing with the hope that Christians will receive this criticism, since it comes from within and not from outside the ranks. I'm writing in order that the observers of the Church who look at it askance may come to know the reality of our faith, and may not view it as an unreal, never-never land.

This is my thesis. Now I must make several qualifying and explanatory statements.

First: I am concerned with a particular segment of the Church. This book is not about outspoken liberals or prominent leaders in some major denominations. Neither is it about the ultra fundamentalists and the extremists on the right.

This book is about those who react against leftist tendencies on the one hand and rightist extremism on the other. It's about Christians, Christians who may call themselves evangelical (some may wish to use the word "fundamental"), Christians who form the strong, vital, middle of Christendom, whatever label they may carry—or refuse to carry. (The word "evangelical" means that which centers in the gospel, the good news of God. Those who are evangelical point to that which God has done *for* man in Jesus Christ, and to that which he can do *in* man through his Spirit.)

Reporting on the First U.S. Congress of Evangelism (September 1969), *Time* magazine estimated that one third of the members of the major denominations are evangelicals. Added to the conservative denominations not affiliated with the National Council of Churches, this would amount to 40 million conservative Protestants—the largest and most determinative block of Christians in the country.

Second: Why write about *them?* I have a sneaking suspicion that more people are nearer the center of Christianity than shout on the noisy fringes. Of course liberals make more noise as they take pot shots at some extremists on the right, and so do the fundamentalists, who are always exposing leftist tendencies they don't happen to like. But who is willing to face the real Church? In a constructive manner, that is?

Third: I write from within the Church, not as an outsider. I was brought into Christianity through evangelical Christians of the highest order, and I enjoyed membership in a conservative Presbyterian Church before becoming a minister of that denomination. I have talked with ministers of all persuasions, but I have held friendships particularly with evangelicals.

As a pastor of three congregations I've come to know many Christians. I hasten to add that this book is *not* about them.

My contacts have been wider than these congregations, and I speak about Christianity at large.

Fourth: I'm not writing out of bitterness. This is not a condemnation of the Church. I write because I love the Church and see the hope of the future not on the right or the left, but in that main stream of evangelical Protestantism. I have been sharp and cutting at times, but always (I hope) realistic.

Some of the things Jesus said alienated him from the religious community of his time. He sounded critical to them, censorious, even abusive. He was ostracized by the religious leaders for his language. And they did sound tough indeed, the words he sometimes spoke:

"What miserable frauds you are, you scribes and Pharisees! You clean the outside of the cup and the dish, while the inside is full of greed and self-indulgence. . . . For you appear like good men on the outside—but inside you are a mass of pretence and wickedness. . . . Your father is the devil . . . you are not sons of God."[2]

Jesus spoke these words to the solid conservatives. They failed, however, to grasp one fact—that behind that harsh language beat a loving heart. As Proverbs 3:12 says: "Whom the Lord loves, he corrects." He spoke as he did because he cared.

There is a possibility, then, that I may be misunderstood by some within the Church for speaking out—and perhaps even ostracized. I'm willing to assume that risk. Let me ask a question, though, one which really bothers me. Why should we hold it all in? Why should we limit our talk about our problems to private conversations or small groups? Everyone has some comments on what's wrong with the Church. Just ask around. You can get a stimulating conversation going on this subject any time.

It is time, then, to be honest and open about ourselves. And I include myself in the sickness which plagues us. I have no intention of aggravating the illness. But if we need radical surgery, that alone will bring about the healing—healing which comes from God.

One final word. To take something apart requires little skill, less education, and still less brains. In that lovable series of Peanuts cartoons (which will emerge more than once in this volume) Lucy makes a little snow man and then kicks him to smithereens. She does it again, while Charlie Brown watches from a distance with a puzzled expression. Another snow man and "pow"! He catches up with her. She explains: "I'm torn between the desire to create and the desire to destroy."

I'm not aiming to kick things apart. Even though the second section of this book speaks frankly of the faults of the Church, the first section lists its strengths. The third (and longest) part offers a modest attempt at reconstruction and renewal. If renewal doesn't take place, I'm afraid that the Church will soon be deserted by all thinking people, a process which, sadly enough, has already begun.

NOTES:

1. Helmut Thielicke, *The Trouble with the Church* (New York: Harper & Row, Inc., 1965), p. 127.
2. Matt. 23:25–28; John 8:44, 47; J. B. Phillips' translation.

What's Right with the Church?

"That the preaching of the gospel might be maintained, God has deposited this treasure with the Church. The Church is the mother of all who have him for their Father."

—John Calvin

"I beg my Church never again to allow itself to be forced into a ghetto. I beg it never to surrender to the powers of this world. I pray that, the harder the life of the Church becomes, the more God may strengthen its spirit of unity, so that it can perceive which things are insignificant and which are important."

—Otto Dibelius

2.
The Place of the Bible

WITH a fury that resembles charging marines on an enemy beach, scholars have for some time battled the Bible. They have attacked holy Scripture with honest efforts and have often left too little for the average Christian to hold on to. In spite of those brilliant maneuvers, evangelical Christians have defended their territory. Sometimes they have done so with a Biblical literalism which repudiated *all* scholarship, as if scholarship belonged to the devil—"nothing good can come from scholars or theologians." This extremism is hardly to the credit of these zealous defenders, yet while Protestants in general have fled from before the fury of the attack, evangelical Christians have maintained their Biblical emphasis.

In June, 1966, a seminar on the authority of the Bible was held at Gordon College in Wenham, Mass. Professors and leaders from all parts of the world studied the meaning of Scripture for our time. A portion of the statement which they adopted reads as follows:

> "Attitudes toward the importance of the Bible are changing throughout the Christian world. The renewal of biblical studies among Roman Catholics and the increasing concern for the biblical message through the whole Church, together with current

> confusions regarding that message, are facts which call for new endeavor on the part of evangelicals. . . .
>
> The Bible is wholly trustworthy, for its words speak God's truth and give men final answers to the deepest problems of their lives. . . . We stand under it and commend it to a frustrated age that needs above all to hear the clear and powerful voice of God in judgment and in grace. . . . Christians have often failed to concern themselves sufficiently with the suffering and injustice of our sick society and hold forth to dying men the Word of Life. We, therefore, give ourselves anew to declaring the biblical Word, which alone offers hope in this world and the next.

This conference which affirmed that the Bible is our only infallible rule of faith and practice illustrates the present adherence of evangelicals to Scripture. Even though new thinking is desperately needed among them in order that they may not become fossilized during current debates, it is apparent that the Bible still remains authoritative.

This steady hammering away at the Bible is not new. Only in recent years the blows have increased. It all began in the garden of Eden (and that was a long time ago!) when the tempter questioned Eve: "Has *God* said, Ye shall not eat of every tree of the garden?"[1] The temptation for man was not an apple, or whatever fruit hung on that forbidden tree, but the question of authority. Has *God* really said that? Is that the word of God? Are you sure he said this to you, or is it merely the figment of your own imagination? Maybe it was just your conscience talking to you? Besides, do you really think God is like that? Posting a sign in the garden, "Thou shalt not eat." Is that what you really believe about God? Don't you think God wants you to enjoy life? Don't you think he wants you to be free, to mature? So, what has God really said to you? What is the word of God? Can it possibly be what you think it is?

The same tempter questioned Jesus in the same way: "If God has said, 'he shall give his angels charge over thee, to keep thee in all thy ways,' and if God has said, 'they shall bear thee up in their hands, lest thou dash thy foot against a stone,' why don't you prove it to yourself? If God makes these promises why don't you take him up on it? Is God like that? Does he really protect you? You will not know what he is like unless you prove it to yourself! Throw yourself down from the temple and get up unharmed. Walk away, and the people will follow you in amazement. Prove to yourself that God will protect you.

"But since you must prove it to yourself, don't you see that you do not really believe? You don't trust God. You don't believe him. Or else you wouldn't have to prove it to yourself. Why do you hesitate? Throw yourself down. Has God not promised to deliver you? What is the word of God to you, Jesus of Nazareth?"[2]

And now through active Biblical research and study, the authority of Scripture has been thrown into question. I do not suggest that scholarship is of the devil. To the contrary, legitimate questions need to be raised honestly. However, Old Testament professors and New Testament scholars have cast doubt on the word of God until all that remains is "scripture when it is scripture for you." That is, the Bible is only the Bible when it speaks directly to you. When you have an existential experience (a personal experience) then God speaks to you. Is this put too crudely? The fact remains that many Christians have followed Adam and Eve into doubt and frustration. Few prefer the reference of Jesus during his time of testing: "It is written . . . it is written again . . . it is written."[3]

Amid this welter of confusion of what Scripture is and what it is not, of what you can believe and what not, the evangelical church has kept a level head. Many a time it has been arrested and pulled over to the curb to answer questions about Jonah and the whale or why the sun stood still for Joshua. In spite of these tactics it has unswervingly maintained that "all scripture is given by inspiration of God," and that "men of God spoke because they were inspired by the Holy Spirit."[4] Nor do evangelicals neglect the living reality of the Word which was in the world: "We are writing to you about something which . . . we had opportunity to observe closely and even to hold in our hands, and yet, as we know now, was something of the very Word of life Himself! For it was *life* which appeared before us."[5]

The word God has spoken to man is recorded in Scripture, but that eternal Word is Jesus Christ come in the flesh. He cannot be known apart from Scripture and the witness of the Holy Spirit. Because of this, it must be said to the credit of the Church that the Scriptures have remained central.

What then do we actually believe about the Bible? Evangelicals wrestle with problems of scholarship. They know what the critics have been saying. Still they may defend the doctrine of inerrancy as Edward J. Young of Westminster Seminary has done in this stimulating paragraph:

> The doctrine of inerrancy for which we contend does not demand the literal interpretation of all parts of Scripture. It does not demand that the writers of the Bible be regarded as mere automata; it does not insist that the writers, whenever they happen to record the same event, must be in actual verbal agreement with one another. . . . Inerrancy does not demand that when two writers translate from another language, their translations should be in verbatim agreement. . . . It does not demand that each writer must view the same event from precisely the same standpoint. Inerrancy, in other words, allows for the full employment of the gifts and talents with which God endowed the human writer. . . . The Bible is a true account . . . one harmonious account of God's gracious plan of redemption. And the reason for this deep unity is to be discovered only in the fact that the Bible is the Word of God.[6]

That such books are circulated indicates among the leadership a desire to maintain a Bible-oriented faith. But this is also true among the people. How often laymen have complained that their minister is not Biblical enough. How often they have said that the sermon was flowery or interesting or enjoyable but not vital. How often they have criticized the sermon for being social, economic or even political without having food from the Bible. How often they have left the churches frustrated because the minister was not true to his calling, to speak forth the word of God.

On the other hand Biblical preaching must have a bite to it. It must make an application to today's world and its problems, or people will leave the church after such a sermon, muttering, "That was very close to the Bible, but it doesn't grab me where I'm living. It didn't really speak to my needs." The Bible can be relevant if we willingly let it be so. It will certainly cry out for application to daily problems in our lives and to our world.

So, there exists among Protestants a desire to hear the Bible expounded and applied to daily life. When others allow the Bible to slip away from them through increasing emphasis on social implications and reform or other matters, many Christians wish to hear the word of God anew. Sometimes such preaching is not handled well. Sometimes it becomes boring, and sometimes its interpreter is so literal that the message remains buried in the time of its writing. All that may be true. But then, too, it can sound forth with a contemporary tone that makes it come alive. Every Christian wants to see this happen. That's what he goes to church for.

A reporter once asked the late actor Charles Coburn how he could keep going in a Broadway play for two years when the dialogue was always the same. How could he keep it fresh?

"Every two months," he replied, "we sit down as an entire cast and read the play as though we had never read or seen it before."

At least one point to be raised about Biblical Christianity is this matter of freshness. How many read their own Bibles and consider it always vital? The Bible keeps fresh because God speaks through his word now. He is the same yesterday, today and always. Perhaps we can keep it from becoming like canned food by reading Scripture "as though we had never read or seen it before."

NOTES:

1. Gen. 3:1.
2. See Matt. 4:1–11 and Psa. 91:11,12.

3. Matt. 4:4,7,10.
4. II Tim. 3:16; II Pet. 1:21 (Phillips).
5. I John 1:1,2 (Phillips).
6. Edward J. Young, *Thy Word Is Truth* (Grand Rapids: Wm. B. Eerdmans Publishing Co., 1957), p. 139. Used by permission.

3.

An Emphasis on Doctrine

> Theology is now a shambles. That is the long and short of it. We have entered a period that has witnessed a massive defection from neo-orthodoxy, the point of view which was dominant during the past three decades. Neo-orthodoxy has been judged for its failure to inspire great preaching . . . for its inability to motivate the church in her mission, and for its failure to give the believer any real understanding of the nature of the struggle that is going on in history. Thus a new generation experiences an absence of meaning in today's world. . . . A theology which has tended to limit God's action either to the past or to the future and has taught that we live in an interim has had little light to shed on the problem of a Christian style of life during this interim.[1]

That was the verdict of the President of Princeton Seminary in 1966.

Someone has said (with tongue in cheek) that doctrine was conceived in Britain, confounded in Germany and corrupted in America. In spite of such confusion and corruption a group in the mainstream of Christianity has always been concerned for *sound* doctrine. They were never led astray by modern trends. They fought the battle against neo-orthodoxy and now that it is passé, they will resist Bultmann's demythologizing as well as the "God is dead movement" of today's theological playboys and whatever innovations are to follow. They believe that the faith once delivered must be maintained.

Evangelical Protestants have contended for this faith by sometimes going beyond the necessary bounds when they made extensive statements of belief. To make sure everything was included in such statements, these often turned out pedantic and elongated like a centipede with too many legs. They have been concerned about the lack of doctrine in the ecumenical movement, where the emphasis is too often on cooperation rather than creed, on unity rather than unadulterated truth. But they have also cast a disdainful glance at the ultra-right, who in their rigidity have failed to be flexible.

It may be to the credit of conservatives to proclaim the whole truth as it runs the gamut from the inspiration of Scripture, the virgin birth, the atoning death of Christ, his resurrection and the coming judgment, to justification and sanctification and all the rest of it. Yet these may be proclaimed without preaching the *whole* counsel of God! The Bible is not silent on the subject of love, nor does it remain mute on the question of injustice. Humility, forgiveness, kindness and patience are part of the word of God. The same apostle who had a great deal to say about justification by faith also wrote the greatest chapter ever written on love.[2] Faithfulness to doctrine is not mere faithfulness to beliefs but to the whole of life.

Doctrines are not to be dissertations on some remote facts, such as trying to discover how many angels can stand on the head of a pin and proclaiming this truth against all errors. Obscure doctrine which delves into the past or future and makes its bed in picayune triviality is about as vital as studying the mating instinct of the gnat. Doctrine must have a bearing on life.

Years ago Phillips Brooks said in his lectures on preaching: "Preach doctrine, preach all the doctrine you know, and learn forever more and more; but preach it always, not that men may believe it, but that men may be saved by believing it."[3]

Who cares what you believe unless it influences your life? True Biblical doctrine will always influence the lives of those who hear it preached.

While Joseph Fort Newton was the minister of the City Temple in London during World War I, he went down to a theater to help in evangelistic services. One night not having heard the sermon, he asked the assembled soldiers what it had been about. One spoke up: "It was on the grace of God. The preacher told us that the grace of God is plentiful, sufficient for all our needs, and near at hand. But he did not tell us what the grace of God is. Perhaps you, sir, will be good enough to do that!"[4] Newton felt upset. He had himself spoken about the grace of God and he had never tried to tell anyone what the word "grace" meant. How great is the possibility of presenting important teaching without either explaining it or applying it! ("Grace" is the love of God, freely given to us who do not deserve it and therefore defined as "unmerited favor.")

What may also happen in the interest of preserving pure doctrine is a resulting narrow fanaticism: "We have the truth and we know it. No one else has it quite like we do." This fashions a narrow bigot who can hardly be to the credit of Christianity.

When Henry Drummond came to America on the invitation of evangelist D. L. Moody, his position on evolution and modern criticism was well known. In fact, Drummond did not identify himself with conservatives and thought he was a bit out of place in Moody's backyard. He came nevertheless, because of the evangelist's gracious insistence. But a delegation confronted Moody and insisted he question Drummond on the soundness of his faith. Some were critical of his smoking cigars and others of his views on the miracles. They threatened not to allow him to speak unless he could satisfy their demands. Moody reluctantly agreed to talk to Drummond.

The next day the delegation met with Moody again.

"Did you see Mr. Drummond?"

"Yes."

"Did you speak to him about his theological views?"

"No, I did not."

"Why not?"

"Within half an hour of his coming down this morning," answered Moody, "he gave me such proof of his being possessed of a higher Christian life than either you or I that I could not say anything to him. You can talk to him yourselves if you like."

Christians of all persuasions need to learn a lesson in humility. After all, the tree is known by its fruit.

We are experiencing a landslide, a falling away from doctrine. Some want peace without problems; ecumenicists emphasize unity irrespective of truth, and liberals voice social action without scriptural proclamation. Amid this avalanche those who hold the fundamentals of the faith need to dig in.

Some want peace without effort, religion made simple, serenity as easy as taking an aspirin and as quick acting as an alkaseltzer. "Now you can find peace of mind in ten minutes," reported the *New York Times*. Rubbish. Our preoccupation with such peace is like an early morning fog. Until it lifts we will never see the mountain peaks of truth.

The ecumenical emphasis on unity lapses into an amalgamation of all things commonly believed with the edges rubbed off. We accumulate a glob of matter, some of which may be very necessary, but everything is thrown in as into Mrs. Murphy's chowder. Some time in the future some will rebel because they will discover the overalls in this ecumenical soup. (And there aren't enough bones in it for flavor.)

The present social involvement program of the Church which entails entanglement in politics, economics, poverty, social issues and the race problem is an earnest attempt to make the Church relevant. But the glaring omissions in this noble effort are the lack of Biblical content. When finally this part of the Church makes contact with our modern world, what does it have to say? Does it have a message? Does it present answers? Or does it merely attempt to raise questions? Too often I have seen only the questions and observed an absence of that gospel which becomes a stumbling block to the wise and foolishness to the intellectual.

> The greatest drag on Christianity today . . . is not the secularism without, it is the reduced Christianity within: the religious generalities and innocuous platitudes of a pallid, anemic Christianity . . . what Kierkegaard called "a vaporized Christianity". . . . This Christianity made easy represents often a sincere and in its own way laudable attempt to construct a bridge between modern culture and the New Testament faith. . . . Yes, indeed: but not at the self-defeating cost of changing Christianity into something else, not at the cost of soft-pedalling the historical-supernatural elements without which Christianity does not exist. . . . This religion of a Jesus who taught wonderful philosophical truths about nature and providence and held views on politics in advance of his time . . . is a poor and watery substitute for the strong and vital faith of the apostles in one who was greater than the prophets. . . .
>
> Is it not time we insisted that . . . a reduced gospel is not only religiously indefensible but even critically unsound? It is bad scholarship, to put it no higher.[5]

"If you believe what you like in the gospel and reject what you like, it is not the gospel you believe, but yourselves."[6]

NOTES:

1. James I. McCord, President of Princeton Seminary, in a letter to ministers, Spring, 1966.
2. I Cor. 13.
3. Quoted by Andrew W. Blackwood, *The Preparation Of Sermons* (New York: Abingdon-Cokesbury, 1948), p. 29. The original source is Phillips Brooks, *Letters on Preaching* (New York: E. P. Dutton & Co.).
4. *Ibid.* 30.
5. James S. Stewart, *A Faith To Proclaim* (New York: Charles Scribner's Sons, 1953), pp. 31–33.
6. St. Augustine.

4.

Evangelical, of Course

IT may seem from the foregoing that a strongly Biblical and doctrinal church has no interest in social issues, in fact that social concern is one thing and evangelical Christianity another. This is not true. A Biblical faith must result in social concern. Wherever it has failed in this, it has shown itself to be inadequate and inconsequential. But should it not be said that such faith produces a high moral tone in Christians which can usually be observed in private as well as public life? What, for example, about the virile emphasis on Christian homes? Those who take Christ seriously do not generally entertain divorce as an idea. (There are instances when divorce becomes inevitable, but these are not as numerable as is popularly supposed.) Recent statistics showed that while one out of three homes in the United States breaks up only one out of forty-seven Christian homes splits up.

Billy Graham speaks of the social obligations of Christians in this manner:

> Christians, above all others, should be concerned with social problems and social injustices. Down through the centuries the Church has contributed more than any other single agency in lifting social standards to new heights. Child labor has been

> outlawed. Slavery has been abolished. The status of women has been lifted to heights unparalleled in history. . . . The Christian is to take his place in society with moral courage to stand up for that which is right, just, and honorable.

Then he proceeds to discuss in detail such specific subjects as "the Christian should be a good citizen, given to hospitality, take a Christian view of marriage, take the Christian attitude in labor-management relationships and economics, look through the eyes of Christ at the race question, and be concerned about suffering humanity around him."[1]

One of the most famous organizations in the world is the result of a man who was evangelical to the core of his being, and therefore a man of Christian charity. William Booth was moved to action and founded the Salvation Army in the slums of London. It is now a one hundred million dollar a year organization with thousands of facilities throughout the world, but whose welfare work is secondary to its religious purposes. Christians who take their Lord seriously offer the love of God on the one hand and hold a cup of cool water in the other.

To say that evangelical Protestants have been evangelical sounds redundant, yet this must be the most important characteristic of those who are convinced that God has entered the world in Jesus Christ. He came to identify himself with man, suffered with us and for us, and rose triumphant from the dead. This good news means salvation for all who will receive him, the Savior of the world! Hence revivals, evangelism, and the seeking of "the lost" have been the hallmark of Protestantism.

The phenomenal growth of the early Church was due to its personal witness. The Reformation was a great awakening in Christendom. The 18th century was influenced by the preaching of Wesley and Whitefield, the 19th century felt the evangelism of Finney and Moody, and the 20th has heard its "Billys" —Sunday and Graham. Millions of Protestants have supported such movements, and particularly is this true of the Graham campaigns. As a result many have become active in their own churches, because they sang, counseled, ushered or brought friends to these meetings.

Such revitalized churches proclaim the good news, and some of their membership are actively engaged in visiting the homes of prospects. These laymen are also vocal wherever they labor or serve. They will do more than speak. They will counsel, help people find jobs, put groceries on the table for needy families, take someone to the hospital, or visit a boy in juvenile hall. They demonstrate Christianity in action, and in this way the poor have the gospel preached to them.

In spite of modern trends in our fast-paced society away from such simple friendliness, the Christian Church considers telling others the good news its prime business. "Go out quickly into the streets and lanes of the city. . . . Go out into the highways and hedges, and compel them to come in."[2] As Jesus sent out the twelve, so have thousands gone out two by two to share the good news that sets men free.

Apart from the Church, there is little good news. It is easy to become disillusioned by the complete wretchedness of mankind, to be overwhelmed by the degradation of fellow human beings. Will man ever change? is a question many people ask. Is the so-called evolution of ethical man a myth; are we instead evolving into more sadistic and selfish creatures?

In answering those questions, many philosophers tend to become aloof in their philosophy. Social workers who begin with the highest aspirations turn out to be the most disappointed: "People don't appreciate what we do for them!" Even psychiatrists delving deeper and deeper into the troubles of human beings may give up on the human race. Are sufficient number ever really changed? What progress—man?

The evolutionists have yielded to the despair of the scientists, for man knowing more than he has ever known is ready to destroy himself. Politicians never had an optimistic view of people to begin with. The words of the Roman poet Horace still echo in our time: "I hate the masses and keep them at a distance." Even religious people can become heartless. The leaders of the Jews said about the common people: "This crowd, who know nothing about the Law, is damned anyway!"[3] This is the pessimism of those who have failed to change others.

"You will come to know men in their wretchedness," was the advice of a mother to her son as he entered the ministry. "Be careful that you never become a cynic." Reinhold Niebuhr once published a book under the fascinating title, *Leaves from the Notebooks of a Tamed Cynic*. Even the great preacher of England, Charles Spurgeon, had moments of despair. He wondered whether his generation was the better for all his preaching and declared once that the world was not worth preaching to!

If anyone ever had a right to become a cynic, it was Jesus. He came from above and not from below.[4] He remained free from sin and human degradation.[5] He knew all men and did not need anyone to tell him what people were like.[6] He knew the miseries of mankind which were due to our rebellious beginnings. He knew what God intended man to be, and how far short that evil and adulterous generation had fallen.[7]

And yet, never does Jesus give way to cynicism. He will not despair of man. Instead he pictures humanity as sheep without a shepherd, lost, lonely and forsaken, seeking its own ways to its own hurt. He prays for workers who will enter into the labors of bringing the sheep into the fold—the fold of which he is the Good Shepherd.[8] Jesus comes to redeem man, to give his life a ransom for many.[9] He comes because he loves. His view of man is certainly realistic but it never overlooks the potential of renewal—Otherwise, why his suffering, agony and death? God's hope for man is restoration.

The Church like her Lord has not given up on mankind, even if everybody else has. She believes in the complete redeemability of any person, which means that no one has sunk so low as to fall beyond the grace of God. If a thief dying on a cross may join Jesus in Paradise, who needs to fear? As the doors of the Union Rescue Mission of Los Angeles proclaim, "There is hope for all who enter here."

Martin Niemöller of Germany had a dream during his imprisonment in a Nazi concentration camp. He dreamed that he saw Hitler pleading his case before God on Judgment Day. Hitler excused himself because he had never heard the gospel. Niemöller listened in amazement. Then he heard a voice directed toward him: "Were you with him a whole hour without telling him of the gospel?" He awoke and remembered that he had indeed been with Hitler for an hour. He had not said a word about Jesus Christ. From that time on Niemöller realized clearly his present duty to witness to all men, even to the guards at the camp.

Such is our opportunity. Generally when men meet, after a casual introduction they ask: "And what's your line?" Well, what is our line? Is it our vocation, our means of making a living? Or is it first and foremost the sharing of our faith? Are we not called to spread the good news of the crucified and risen Lord? Many of us feel this is our true vocation, and our business is merely the means of making a living.

On a theatre marquée announcing one of those risqué movies, the sign read: "For unashamed adults only." The message of salvation should not make anyone ashamed, since it is God's power for redemption to anyone who believes. The sharing of it is not only our duty but a God-given privilege. Unashamed Christians have been the light of the world as they have brought the good news to the not-yet-Christian world. It is a world that Jesus loves and has died for:

> The world He suffered to redeem;
> For all He hath the atonement made;
> For those that will not come to Him
> The ransom of His life was paid.[10]

If this has been too glowing a picture, then when we think of what's wrong with the church, that will surely correct any such overstatement. But it must be stated positively that one of the strengths of evangelical Christianity is its desire to "get the message out." For "God was in Christ personally reconciling the world to himself—not counting their sins against them—and has commissioned us with the message of reconciliation. We are now Christ's ambassadors, as though God were appealing direct to you through us. As his personal representatives we say, 'Make your peace with God.' "[11]

As D. T. Niles has so well put it, "Evangelism is simply one beggar telling another beggar where the bread is to be found."

The Christian is not above the not-yet-Christian. He lives in a sinful world as one who is neither to be superior nor proud. He knows, however, how our hunger for righteousness may be filled—with "the bread of God which comes down from heaven and gives life unto the world."[12] And that bread is worth sharing.

NOTES:

1. Billy Graham, *Peace With God* (New York: Doubleday & Company, 1953), pp. 190–199. Copyright 1953 by Billy Graham. Reprinted by permission of Doubleday & Company, Inc.
2. Luke 14:21,23.
3. John 7:49 (Phillips).
4. John 8:23.
5. John 8:46.
6. John 2:25.
7. Matt. 12:39.
8. Matt. 9:36–38.
9. Mark 10:45.
10. Charles Wesley.
11. II Cor. 5:19,20 (Phillips).
12. John 6:33.

5.

Missionary Passion

THE earliest and simplest creed of Christianity was "Jesus Christ is Lord."[1] As Christ's servants we obey him. Sometimes our obedience has turned into an overemphasis whereby Christians have become obsessed with duty and begun to act as slaves. Thus the equally valid truth that God is our Father and we are his children becomes obscured. Being a slave is hardly the same as enjoying the relationship of a son. Nevertheless, the lordship of Christ has at times resulted in outstanding Christian commitment.

Take as an example the financial support given to the church and its mission. In the United States, churches largely support themselves and send missionaries everywhere as well. In many countries denominations are supported by the state and there is hardly any emphasis on stewardship. Evangelicals emphasize tithing, which means giving one-tenth of one's income. That is a sizable chunk. (Some would debate whether it is on gross or net income, but if it turns out to be net, how much is that whittled down?) In some mainline denominations tithing is hardly ever mentioned, and then if it is, only gingerly—as if we shouldn't ask for that much. But many Christians give this amount (and more) as a return in recognition that *all* belongs to God.

The more evangelical the church, the higher the per capita giving! Figures show that the per capita giving of such smaller groups as the Free Methodists, the Reformed Presbyterians and the Covenant Church are sometimes twice that of the Episcopalians, the Methodists and the Churches of Christ. "Money people" do not necessarily turn out to be the most generous contributors; in fact, many low income families by their regularity outgive their Christian brethren. Why? Because their lives are committed to Jesus Christ, and they desire to serve the One who has given himself for us all.

A very young Christian (although physically he is in his forties) once wrote me: "I lost $25 betting at the racetrack last week. So if I can lose it at the racetrack, I can do no more than send the same to my church. Seems to me, we can spend anything on pleasure and then slip in 50¢ to church." He's on his way to a more mature faith, for sending that $25 was quite a sum for him. He probably had never given that much to a church before.

Consider also the stewardship of missions. In spite of the fact that the Protestant Church spends less on its missionary program than the nation spends on dog food, who else has manifested missionary concern? The mission of the Church is mission: "We must go with Christ to the frontiers of this nation and the frontiers of the world, or part with Christ in our sanctuaries at home."[2] The entire missionary movement springs from the word of God. The thousands of missionaries who have gone and who even now witness everywhere in the world are the testimony of a Church that cares, a Church which has responded to God's word.

F. W. Robertson has pointed out that whereas the spirit of Judaism was separation, the spirit of Christianity has been permeation. The Jews separated evil from good, one nation from all other nations, certain meats from other foods, certain days from other days. On the other hand Christianity permeates evil with good and aims at overcoming evil with good. It takes seriously the words of Jesus that "the kingdom of Heaven is like yeast, taken by a woman and put into three measures of flour until the whole lot had risen."[3] It hopes to transfuse the spirit of one day of rest and worship into the remainder of the week. So also it hopes to bring the good news to every nation and to saturate life with the presence of God.

President Franklin D. Roosevelt is reported to have said: "Since becoming President, I have come to know that the finest of Americans we have abroad today are the missionaries of the cross. I am humiliated that I am not finding out until this late day the worth of foreign missions and the nobility of the missionaries."

Charles Malik, Lebanese ambassador to the United Nations, asked in a speech: "What has been the greatest American contribution to the rest of the world? Has it been money? Has it been food? Has it been medical skill? Has it been military might? Has it been industrial know-how?" Then he answers: "The greatest thing to come out of America has been the American missionary effort: the quiet, selfless men and women who have left the comfort and security of their homeland to bring the gospel of Christianity to less favored nations."

A surgeon from Baltimore left a $45,000 a year practice to serve as a medical missionary in an Alaskan outpost for $3000. Such dedication is not uncommon in the Church. Others have given a year of service after perhaps working in their profession for twenty years, going to Korea, South America, or Africa without any financial remuneration. They have shared their skills and taught medicine, engineering, or agriculture. These men never make the front pages. Only a few hear their stories of dedication. And who really grasps what missionaries endure in privation, sacrifice or loss of "the American way of life"? They will only make front page reading on the other shore.

Nothing of course is easier for a novelist or playwright than to jeer at those simple missionaries or tell a spicy story of one such lonely person who went wrong. Of course there are failures. Not even the Christian missionary movement has scored one hundred percent success! Nevertheless in a straightforward critique of the missionary movement, author and translator J. B. Phillips writes this glowing, personal account:

> I read letters from overseas. Here I can breathe the fresh air, the air in which there is the unmistakable tang of the moving Spirit of God. . . . There are setbacks and disappointments, difficulties and even disasters enough to make the angels weep. But—to my mind at least—among this far-flung scattered army of the men and women of Christ there flourish the same gay courage, the same unconquerable loyalty as I found in the history of the Young Church.
>
> I have never been a missionary myself, but I grasp with both hands the opportunity of paying tribute to this magnificent, unadvertised army. I know many missionaries personally, and . . . I believe there is no body of people who more deserve our respect, our admiration and our support.[4]

I need only to add that through new methods in our time we have sought to present the good news through radio, television and the Scriptures translated into many languages. Many charges can be made against some outlandish, hackneyed and miserable broadcasts, but there are also a few noble efforts. Christian stations established throughout the world have sometimes enjoyed good success. A missionary in the southern part of India reported that during his last two years he experienced more conversions than during his entire twenty years previously. People came from villages looking for him and asking about Christianity. Their first bits of information had come through Christian radio.

Any Sunday—and in certain areas during the week as well—you can turn your dial to many an amateurish gospel broadcast. Good or bad, the question must still be asked—who pays for all this? How do these programs support themselves? (And some manage a fairly prosperous living from this, too!) Who else but evangelical Christians foot the bill? These Christians believe in telling the old-yet-ever-new story of Jesus and his love.

Surely then, on the plus side of Christianity we can hardly omit the consecrated men and women who have taken the lordship of Christ seriously and brought the good news to the ends of the earth. Some even in this century have paid for their faith by their blood.

NOTES:

1. Phil. 2:11.
2. John A. Mackay.
3. Matt. 13:33 (Phillips).
4. J. B. Phillips, *The Church Under The Cross* (New York: The Macmillan Company, 1956), x–xi.

6.
Sincerity

TO speak of sincerity in the Church will act like a buffer before we turn to what happens to be wrong. There are many sincere Christians who have no desire of playing the hypocrite and who want very much to live good lives. I must say from my observation that few people strive to be consciously insincere. To question the sincerity of Christians seems hardly necessary.

In spite of their sincerity, Christians may slip into sin. They fail. They are not the accomplished models of perfection which some expect the churches to turn out. And yet, their very sincerity is a monument to their faith. They are the quiet people who humbly and unobtrusively serve Jesus Christ, and of whom he said that of such is the kingdom of God.

The movies often portray the hero as an accomplished, successful person, the model of perfection. We desire to be like him, strong, virile, in command, magnificent. He never makes a mistake. But he is out of reach! In a wax museum in Southern California are portrayed heroes and heroines in all their splendor—perfect specimens of humanity. They look beautiful and handsome and as though they were doing everything just right. Caught in these poses they appear to be real enough, but they cannot move. They are not alive. They are in the *wax* museum. They are dummies. With never a flaw in their make up they do not reveal deformities of figure, tired lines under the eyes, a nervous twitch in the cheek, or the weariness and boredom of living. The perfection of the wax covers up the thousand and one things that keep real people from achieving perfection, to say nothing of hiding their mind, their motives and their temptations.

Unfortunately we do expect Christian models of perfection. Yet these cannot exist in the flesh and blood. At the same time it is possible to be sincere and genuine. The sincerity of which I speak is the kindness of Christians who regularly take flowers from the sanctuary to the shut-ins and sick, and all without a word of complaint; glad to do it and sincerely willing to serve. The sincerity of which I speak is the willingness to go at a moment's notice to visit a family in need, to talk to them in their time of stress and perhaps shop for groceries at a neighborhood market—to be a friend to some who may be newcomers in the city, extending help in the name of Christ.

The sincerity of which I speak is the openness of a family to take into their home a person who may be mentally disturbed or who may need to find again the moorings of life in a secure home situation. Such a Christian family, not expecting pay, sincerely cares. And to the confused or disturbed, their light will always shine.

Or, this sincerity may be seen in the simple way Christians work on their church boards, teach in their Sunday schools, sing in their choirs or perhaps paint the church building when it needs it, giving their time freely. Nothing spectacular, but when people do not have to be coerced and prodded into serving, it is a joy to behold.

I am quite aware that this sounds like a glowing picture. (I only wish I could say this of the many rather than of the few that come to my mind.) But no one can move around among the churches for very long without realizing that some of the finest people in the world are in their ranks. Good people, down-to-earth people, sincere.

It is possible, of course, to fake sincerity. Even unconsciously. John Marquand makes that one point throughout his novel about a character named Willis Wayde:

> Willis dominated the scene, modestly and sincerely. His ease was the best thing about him. You could not tell . . . how much of his cordiality was real. There was no way of gauging the depth of his sincerity. It might very well have been that he did have a soft spot in his heart, and that he had honestly meant what he had said about loyalty, and about being deeply sorry. On the other hand he might have had no heart at all! Authority and success made him strangely impervious, since success had smoothed down all his rough edges. . . .
>
> "Why darling," Sylvia said, "you don't have to wonder anything like that, because you've always been wonderful. No one knows better than I do how wonderful you've been."
>
> Willis cleared his throat. Even though he liked what she said, it was a time to face facts.
>
> "That's very sweet of you to say so . . . but occasionally it's seemed to me you've had a few reservations. God knows I've tried to do a lot of things the right way. . . . I've tried to be sincere . . . I really have—in all my dealings, but sometimes it's a problem—how to be sincere."
>
> "I know you've always tried, dear," Sylvia said.[1]

What a penetrating and probing analysis! But there is also a sincerity which cannot be faked. It comes from having confidence in people and approaching them without fear of being stabbed in the back. You can sense a goodness which radiates from such a person.

It must be said to the credit of evangelicals that when others sneer at the word "pious" and pooh-pooh the necessity of a holy life, these Christians retain a balance between belief and behavior. They realize that ceremony is useless unless conduct is affected and that "pious" is not a nasty word. The impact of that singular life of Jesus was due not simply to his theology but to the magnetism of his godly life. He lived what he believed.

Our present emphasis on social involvement should never become a substitute for this divine dimension. After all, the man of the world expects something from Christians. He may even expect more from us than we do from ourselves! He has often been disappointed, but he will certainly not be impressed when we play down the value of saintliness. He is actually searching for some of that sincerity and trustworthiness which is so woefully absent in the commercial world. He sometimes wonders whether there is any decency anywhere!

In one of his sermons, Peter Marshall told of the people he counseled in his ministry who told him shocking stories—often, as he said, "without any sense of guilt or conviction of sin at all"—that would rock him to the depths of his soul. And he began to wonder if anywhere in the country there remained any real decency and purity.[2]

All of us may have wondered this at times. Yet Peter Marshall also knew those sincere, honest folk who were the backbone of his church. When Jesus told the apostles that they were "the salt of the earth," he was speaking to a group of very ordinary fellows.[3] He did not address the rich or successful, politicians or educators, economists or scientists, spacemen or entertainers, nor was he thinking of clergymen. The ones who know how to live for the kingdom of God will preserve society. They will keep it from rotting by living humbly, showing mercy, making peace, striving for purity of heart, and hungering for more of God. "How happy are the humble-minded, for the kingdom of Heaven is theirs!"[4]

No substitute can be found for such Christians. No one can take their place. Nicolas Berdyaev, who abandoned Marx for Kant and then Kant for Christianity, insists that neither history nor theology or the church brought him to the Christian faith, but a simple woman called Mother Maria. He was present when the Nazis liquidated the Jews in gas chambers. One distraught mother refused to part with her baby. When Maria saw that the officer was only interested in the correct numbers, without a word she pushed the mother aside and quickly took her place. This deed revealed to the philosopher the heart of Christianity. As it does to us!

‡ ‡ ‡

I could continue to list the good points of the Church, but such is not my purpose. Besides, enough is enough. I have attempted to indicate that all is not lost. There is strength in the Church, as long as Christians are Biblical, doctrinal, evangelistically concerned, missionary in purpose and desiring to live sincerely. In spite of all that is wrong, whenever Christians want to *be* Christian in word and deed, hope remains.

NOTES:

1. John Marquand, *Sincerely, Willis Wayde* (New York: Little Brown & Co. 1955), pp. 409, 415, 416.
2. Peter Marshall, *Mr. Jones Meet The Master* (Old Tappan, New Jersey: Fleming H. Revell Company, 1952), p. 132.
3. Matt. 5:13.
4. Matt. 5:3 (Phillips).

What's Wrong with the Church?

"If you want to preach the gospel and help people, you must be sharp and rub salt into their wounds, showing the reverse side and denouncing what is not right."

—Martin Luther

"You know what the trouble with you is, Charlie Brown?" asks Lucy.

"No; and I don't want to know! Leave me alone!"

Charlie Brown walks away angry, hands in his pockets.

Lucy calls after him: "The whole trouble with you is you won't listen to what the whole trouble with you is!"

—Charles M. Schulz

7.

So Easily Contented

WHEN E. Stanley Jones was a missionary in India, he often found himself in the embarrassing situation of having to defend Christianity. As he presented Jesus to the people of other faiths, he was frequently slapped with the question: "Why are you Christians not more like your Christ?" The questioners were unwilling to become Christians because of what they had seen or failed to see in Christians.

Two missionaries went to the Arab world and were greeted by a shouting, spitting mob who called out: "The deceivers! There go the deceivers!" After twenty years in that particular area, Christianity could claim only twenty-seven converts. And that was supposed to be a good record for the Arab world. Would it have been more if Christians were more like their Christ?

We may pacify ourselves with the fact that Jesus didn't make everyone a Christian either. But that's not good enough. When the Moslem says of a drunk that he has left Mohammed and gone over to Jesus, we cannot sit back content. And it is not Jesus' fault, that's for sure. When the Hindu raises the stinging question why we are not like our Christ, we can't shrug that off either. It's about time we listen.

The fact is that the Christian Church as a whole is not like

Jesus. Of course, there are a few people who are trying to be. We have all met them—the people who are the last to describe themselves in those terms, who are struggling, trying to be like Christ. But many more are quite content to remain as they are, wherever that happens to be.

A strange contradiction looms in the Church between the fervency of doctrine and its application to life. Christians believe in the power of God. Preaching salvation through Christ, they hold to the transforming power of God's Spirit. "Therefore if any man be in Christ, he is a new creature: old things are passed away; behold, all things are become new,"[1] is a favorite quote. It seems much easier to quote it, however, than to put it into practice.

Are Christians really made new? Does the newness show? Is the change reality? Or is it mostly talk? When such questions are raised, contented Christians shrug their shoulders and say that the questions don't apply—not to them. "We are not perfect, that's for sure, but we are certainly not a stumbling-block to those outside the Church either." No, they consider themselves the good, solid believers. Those Moslems or Hindus or Americans who criticize the Church are not talking about them—but about all those other hypocritical or liberal Christians.

A few years ago I attended a luncheon for Jews and Christians interested in Israel. Mrs. Helen Gahagen Douglas was seated at our table. In the course of the conversation she criticized two ministers who were to travel to the Holy Land. They had told her they would walk around the sea of Galilee and Mrs. Douglas commented that they were not the kind that would do what they said. None at the table knew that I was a Christian minister and no other minister seemed to be present, for as the discussion continued those people came to the conclusion that very few ministers—less than half—emulated the life of Jesus.

The time has come for evangelicals to listen to what other people think of us!

Most missionaries who go to other lands are firm believers. They have something to give because they have experienced something. And they know what that something is. Their conservatism compels them to preach the good news. In spite of the many splendid missionaries, the question must still be raised why the entire missionary movement has failed so miserably in the world. Why has it failed to stop the onward march of Communism? Why has it failed to establish a strong Christian Church in many lands? Why is the Church in the world financially inadequate, numerically insignificant and socially irrelevant? Why are Christians in foreign lands often scarcer than words of praise from a selfish fellow?

Why in our Western world has Christianity been dismissed by so many? Why are the churches emptying in Europe and even in some parts of the United States? Why have so many moderns turned away from Christianity? Is this the fault of God? Has Jesus failed to be convincing? Is it the shortcoming of the Holy Spirit? Surely the fault lies with us Christians who blandly overlook all our own faults and can only see them in the other fellow. We fail to examine our own lives and manage somehow to evade all responsibility for development in our faith. We are content to be what we are and see no need for change. We are not a scandal and think ourselves to be good examples.

In this proud state of mind we never take criticism seriously. Why should we? They're not talking about us, are they? They're talking about those others. It's just like some of those sermons we hear. They're meant for Joe.

Someone says that men will make all sorts of allowances for a pretty girl. Women will make all sorts of allowances for an unmarried man. But for too long we have been making allowances for mediocre Christians. There is hardly any emphasis on "holy living" within Christianity. During the monastic era the Church emphasized separation and devotion to God, but ever since the doctrinal pounding of the seventeenth century, *creed* has emerged stronger than *conduct*. No one wants to go back to the Middle Ages, but surely a good balance of both emphases is in order.

On the other hand in the ecumenical movement the cry is for unity. The concern is for an application of the message to the great social issues of our time. As a result "pietism" has become a naughty word. Even within evangelical circles there is hardly any sustained preaching on what William Law once called "a serious call to a devout and holy life."

There are devotional books galore. But they are extremely thin in content and more bent on imparting true doctrine than discussing disciplined living. The books in our century which deal with purity of heart are few and far between. W. E. Sangster's *The Pure in Heart,* which is now out of print, seems to be one of the last of this line. Such matters as discipline and holiness are simply passé.

With this gaping neglect on Christlike living, it is any wonder that the average Christian has a rather good feeling about himself? He cannot see any great lack. He is never shown a goal. He has been saved, and therefore he must be good enough for heaven. What does he need more? *As long as you are content why should you have to become something you already think you are?*

"The only tragedy in the world is the tragedy of not being a saint," said Leon Bloy. Most Christians, then, are living tragic lives.

When I went to my first church, I expected to find heaven on earth. I thought that these people would live like Christians, be kind to one another, understand, forgive, love—in short, exemplify the life of Christ in all their relationships. Perhaps I expected to find people who were better Christians than I was since I had only become one two and a half years earlier. (I took on this pastoral responsibility while still a student in seminary.)

I did not walk into a Christian utopia. I was in fact disturbed by what I found, and have kept on finding. Every conceivable form of outward misconduct was present in that community; even more shocking were the petty jealousies, the hurt feelings, the tempers, the unforgiving attitudes, and the pride that got in the way of Christian love. Sins of the flesh and sins of the spirit.

I am not swinging into the lane of perfectionism. I do not

now expect perfection, nor believe it possible. In those days I had a large dose of idealism. It was obviously misplaced idealism because of what I expected from Christianity and Christians. The nature of man, including Christians, is such that he lives only by the grace of God. What does this really mean? It means that grace is never needed where sin is absent. If we are to live by God's forgiving love (grace) we need to be aware that there is something to forgive! If, therefore, we could reach perfection, we would no longer need the grace of God.

But this is no reason to throw out the word "pietism" or forget about our goals. When anyone of us attempts to compare himself with Jesus, he cannot help but be aware of the infinite distance which remains. Only the most arrogant Christian would identify himself with the humble Christ. Bishop Stephen Neill says in a chapter entitled "The Perfectionist Error": "So subtle is sin that genuine victory over certain forms of it may itself contribute the temptation to fall into other and less obvious forms. The claim to perfection can all too easily lead to arrogance and self-sufficiency, to harsh criticism of other Christians, to a sense of superiority."[2] And so on and so forth.

"The measure of the Church's success is God's love in Jesus Christ reflected in us and to one another."[3] The scandal of Christianity is that so few even desire to approach this kind of success. Most of us accept correct beliefs and fight like bears for them, but neglect Christian behavior. And often, the more we talk about God, the less we do about living for him. Faith is underlined in heavy print and works are given a footnote. What is needed is proper balance, a change of emphasis. Even though Protestants hold to both faith and works, like a seesaw we have weighted down the one end, allowing the other to remain up in the air.

The first step to regaining balance is that we must become aware of our own blindness. We must not shove the blame on everybody else, or be unwilling to admit that anything is wrong with ourselves. A little humility will go a long way, and we Christians are in need of it. Talking about humility is not the same as being humble. The time has come to quit our rocking-chair habit of being satisfied and contented.

NOTES:

1. II Cor. 5:17.
2. Stephen Neill, *Christian Holiness* (New York: Harper & Row, Inc., 1960), p. 37.
3. Eugene Carson Blake.

8.
So Critical

GOVERNOR Giles of Virginia once wrote a note to Patrick Henry, in which he demanded satisfaction: "Sir, I understand that you have called me a 'bob-tail' politician. I wish to know if it be true; and if true, your meaning."

To which Patrick Henry replied: "Sir, I do not recollect having called you a bob-tail politician at any time, but think it probable I have. Not recollecting the time or occasion, I can't say what I did mean, but if you will tell me what you think I meant, I will say whether you are correct or not. Very Respectfully, Patrick Henry."

Criticism is universal and can be extremely damaging. Unfortunately, not everyone can wriggle out of the effects as cleverly as Patrick Henry. Yet we continue to indulge. Perhaps we can understand the enthusiasm of Lady Britomart, "whose conscience is clear and her duty done when she has called everybody names."[1] But why should *Christians* behave in this manner? Why do we expect others to stumble and, when they do, why do we gloat over their failures? *I told you so,* we say. *I knew it would happen to her. Didn't I tell you?*

From very new Christians we may expect a certain amount of critical spirit. There remains still so much of the old life that the new has not been affected. We will not be overly surprised at a young Christian's attitude when he goes to church and sees that group of his neighbors he has hitherto avoided. His mind flits "to and fro between an expression like 'the body of Christ' and the actual faces in the next pew." If "any of those neighbours sing out of tune, or have boots that squeak, or double chins, or odd clothes," he will criticize instead of worship and consider "their religion . . . somehow ridiculous."[2]

But why are mature Christians so critical? Why should this tendency deepen in their lives? We dare not excuse ourselves that since everybody else is critical, we have a right to be like that also. That will never do. A Christian is supposed to be living a new life. Should not this critical spirit be removed? How can it be done?

C. S. Lewis gives us a big clue when he raises the obvious question: "If I, being what I am, can consider that I am in some sense a Christian, why should the different vices of those people in the next pew prove that their religion is mere hypocrisy and convention?"[3]

Perhaps if we take our eyes off the other person and begin to examine ourselves, more will begin to happen than has yet happened. We criticize because we are comparing, always comparing, instead of turning our eyes within. As a Christian do I not take my stand as an unworthy person before Christ? As a Christian do I not admit my own failures in confession? Then, how can I even begin to think about anyone else? Do I even have time for this luxury? And if I have time, why don't I spend it more profitably on my own faults? If, therefore, Christ has made a difference in my life, how can I constantly allow all this vicious talk out of my mouth?

Someone has described a fundamentalist as "too much fun and too much damn and too little mentality." That may not be kind, but this is no time for kindness. When we damn everybody else, we only bring trouble on ourselves. Jesus taught this: "With what judgment you judge, you shall be judged."[4]

We generally judge people by drawing a horizontal line at eye level. Those who come up to our line, we approve of. Those who fall below the line, we disapprove. We go about every day putting others below that line including our friends, people we meet, and people in the churches. If a man can measure up, he's fine. If he doesn't, he's an undesirable or a bum. Who has a right to make this standard? By what authority do we set ourselves up as judges? Are we really in any position to make such judgments?

"If you cannot make yourself such an one as you would, how will you be able to have another in all things to your liking? In judging of others a man labors in vain, often errs, and easily sins, but in judging and examining himself, he always labors fruitfully."[5]

We become what we are because of our lack of self-examination. When we cannot forgive, we have failed to see ourselves as forgiven sinners. To *really* see ourselves—that way is the only way back. Then our glaring inconsistencies become obvious, particularly when we examine ourselves by the true standard. The horizontal line which proceeds from our own selves keeps us in good standing. But it is too pat. The Biblical standard is something else. It is vertical—the life of Jesus. This is how life should be lived.

Edmund Steimle told in a radio sermon[6] of a Jewish tailor and his Christian wife. Shortly after the end of World War II, the tailor said to him: "Mr. Steimle, I have a problem. As you know I am a Jew and my wife is a Christian. Her brother was a violent Nazi. When we were in Germany he hated me and did nothing to help us. Now he is in a prison camp and he has written, asking us to send him some food. My wife says no. We send him nothing. But I say yes, we should send him something. What do you think?" To which Steimle commented that he felt humbled and ashamed because of that "Christian" wife.

"For Christ suffered for you and left you a personal example, and wants you to follow in his steps. He was guilty of no sin nor the slightest prevarication. Yet when he was insulted he offered no insult in return. When he suffered he made no threats of revenge. He simply committed his cause to the one who judges fairly."[7] If this is indeed our example, how does it happen that we have missed the boat so badly?

Have Christians actually read such passages as these: "You sit and speak against your brother; you slander your own mother's son. These things you have done and I have been silent; you thought that I was one like yourself." "Let there be no more resentment, no more anger or temper, no more violent self-assertiveness, no more slander and no more malicious remarks. Be kind to one another; be understanding. Be as ready to forgive others as God for Christ's sake has forgiven you."[8]

Perhaps part of our trouble is also that we have made what we term salvation in Christ so all important, that everything else has faded into insignificance. We have put our conception of the gospel ("you are saved by grace through faith")[9] in the Number One spot, and the words of Jesus, "Judge not that you be not judged,"[10] way down the line, almost as an appendix. It comes so much later that you can take it or leave it, as you like it.

Although we don't dare to say it this way, we think if we can only get people saved, this is what really counts. Whether they stop being critical doesn't matter too much. That's really up to them. At least, it's not the gospel. It isn't? Why not? What is the gospel? Isn't it to be set free from our sinful ways and habits? Isn't it to receive new life in Christ for now and eternity? Do we not want to hear about liberation from our critical, self-centered spirits? Are we so bound up within ourselves that "gospel" only means getting our souls saved but not our nasty tempers controlled?

The gospel is supposed to have some positive effect on my life. To be saved is to follow Christ. How then can I still climb the throne of judgment to let my criticisms be carried far and wide when I am one on whom God has had mercy? A true experience of God's mercy should so humble me that occupying the throne of judgment no longer lures me. God accepted me when I was poor and needy, and I am still so. "Blessed are the poor in spirit. . . ."[11] This is what the gospel means. So, perhaps we need to look again at the very meaning of the word "salvation" and its resultant freedom.

An influential pastor of a large church openly criticized a member of one of his committees. The person had failed to do a certain job and had not shown up for the meeting. The pastor was irritated. He spoke out in what was hardly a Christlike manner. What he said was true, but that did not make it right.

When he arrived home he tried to pray, but his own unforgivable behavior at the committee began to bother him. He realized he had torn down another Christian in front of his friends. He became so disturbed that he sat down to write a letter to every committee member, asking them to forgive him. In these eight letters he also asked for their prayers. Will that minister be quick to judge at the next committee meeting, or anywhere else for that matter?

Writing those letters was not easy to do. But why do we always expect everything to be easy in Christianity? The way that leads to life is narrow—not like the broad easy road coasting down hill all the way. Self-examination is painful; that is why we shun it. But the way to deal with a critical spirit is to bring oneself into the presence of Christ.

Do we take this matter seriously? Do we consider it "gospel"? We must. We cannot be made whole unless we are willing to face this ugly pettiness about ourselves!

NOTES:

1. G. B. Shaw.
2. C. S. Lewis, *The Screwtape Letters* (New York: The Macmillan Company, 1945), p. 16.
3. *Ibid.*, p. 18.
4. Matt. 7:2.
5. *The Imitation Of Christ.*
6. Edmund Steimle over the Protestant Hour.
7. I Pet. 2:21–23 (Phillips).
8. Psa. 50:20,21, RSV; Eph.4:31,32 (Phillips).
9. Eph. 2:8.
10. Matt. 7:1.
11. Matt. 5:3.

9. Rigid

A RESISTANCE to change seems to be built into the very structure of our churches. We cling to the past. We cannot bear to let go of nineteenth-century practices in the twentieth century. Some churches have traditionally held services Sunday morning and evening, with a prayer meeting on Wednesday, not to mention all the other regularly scheduled meetings. To change from these would be tantamount to heresy. "We have always done things this way," we say, "and we will continue to do them this way. Why should we change? Besides, the prayer meeting is the backbone of the church." Some churches have some pretty weak backbones, but the skeleton is still there, and the feeling is, *don't let's ever change; let's remain the way we are.*

I have heard it said that if you decide to change the position of the organ pipes or move the baptismal font or decide to get rid of a poor stained glass window, "all hell" will break loose in the congregation. And it will, too. At some meetings with the elders I have sat back in amazed silence while matters I considered serious and important were voted on without hesitation, and minute items ate up hours of discussion.

Such attitudes may all be reaction. The world is changing so rapidly. Everything is coming loose. We are moving with such speed through time and into space that every new invention throws us off guard. We hear of changes in some churches and they scare us. Some ministers are leaving their pulpits for jobs in the Peace Corps, the anti-poverty program, the Job Corps, or other social-oriented specialized jobs. They explain that they can better minister in such organizations. The most notable example of this considerable number who feel the Church has had it, is the former California Bishop, James A. Pike. At the age of fifty-three he joined the Robert M. Hutchins Center for the study of Democratic Institutions. I am not advocating this kind of change.

Nor do I plead for all those new approaches where church services are held on the beach in bathing trunks, or a minister hires a boat to say prayers with fishermen on a lake. And that may be all right for those who do it, but it's hardly a recommended practice for all. So many radical approaches are being tried in both the world and in the Church that the solid old-time Christians are loath to change. In a way we cannot blame them—they want to preserve the Church.

On the other hand, what are we really preserving? Perhaps it is time to gain insight from the creative methods of those who minister in apartment houses and industrial complexes, or through coffee houses strategically located, reaching the hitherto unreached or unreachable. At least if they are willing to try some new ideas, evangelicals will have something to say when they get there. It really would be quite in order to chuck a poorly attended Sunday evening or Wednesday service to make room for some new approach that would reach new faces.

Why this resistance to change? Must the Church repeat her past blunders, as for example, when she held onto traditions and fought Galileo? As for doing what we have always done because we have always done it, who can actually prove that we have *always* done it? Were such conventions as the Sunday school, youth groups, evening services or the extensive organizational machinery of our local churches part of the apostolic program? That is not to say they are all worthless, but we must remember that most of our accepted practices come from the nineteenth century. We can hardly claim that we have always done it that way.

We will have the same sort of eye-opener when we realize that many of the popular gospel hymns are not "the grand, old hymns of the Church," but are usually not even a hundred years old. Such hymns as "I Need Thee Every Hour," "Take Time To Be Holy," and "Have Thine Own Way, Lord," were written in 1872, 1895 and 1907 respectively. The old hymns are ones like "A Mighty Fortress" (1529), "Now Thank We All Our God" (1636), and "Jesus, the Very Thought of Thee" (a translation from an eleventh-century Latin poem).

Churches still holding evening services notice their attendance continually slipping. Mostly only the old regulars attend because they feel they ought to keep it going. When a movie is shown in some churches the attendance doubles, except where the movie fad has worn off. What does this really say about such services? What sort of farce is this? Wednesday evening is usually a more pitiful story. So few show up that if the old prayer meeting has not lost its vitality, it has certainly lost its numbers.

This same rigidity can also be observed in regard to behavior. We have carried over from Puritan times a series of restrictions which mark the good Christians as those who do not play cards, dance, drink, smoke, gamble, attend movies, wear make-up, etc., or (depending on the group) any variation of these, add or take away a few. This new legalism supposedly identifies the good Christians.

Years ago in England the Puritans actually succeeded in getting adultery included among the crimes punishable by death. Some were hanged for the offense. Then the inevitable happened. Juries refused to convict and the law became a dead letter. In our own time society would never tolerate this sort of interference, but has swung to the other extreme of permissiveness. Twentieth-century society places no limitations on our freedom.

Our refusal to change the patterns in the Church may again be a reaction to the trend of society. I am not pleading for a relaxation of all standards, nor do I desire to bring about license within the churches. But the rigid attitude which refuses to change the customary or what may in reality be only a *church's* commandment, needs to be examined. Are the matters we hold on to more tightly than an octopus clings to its prey of Christ or of man? Can we afford to make the same mistakes as the Pharisees when they clung to their traditions and pushed aside the law of God? They never *thought* they were guilty of that of course, until Jesus pointed it out. They had substituted their own traditions for God's will.[1] Must we not examine all our customary observances and prohibitive restrictions in that light?

> The Fundamentalist attitude toward dancing, movies, and wine often takes an extreme form. These are by nature evil, some say; they are always and everywhere to be resisted. . . . What it condemns may indeed be used evilly, but that does not mean that it is evil in and of itself. There is nothing intrinsically evil about the camera or dancing or wine. . . .
>
> The Fundamentalist catalogue of "sins" is small and specific. . . . No " spiritual Christian" will presumably do any of these things, and generally will have little to do with anyone who does do them. Everyone who grows up in this tradition finds that it has a vise-like grip on him. . . . If he "weakens" and indulges, he is filled with guilt-feelings as automatically as Pavlov's dog salivated when the bell rang. . . .
>
> It is against this mind-set in Fundamentalism that the writer wishes to protest. He is not arguing for drinking, for smoking, for dancing, for gambling, even for movie-attendance. But he is concerned lest Christians confuse ethical living with an arbitrary legalistic bondage. He is concerned lest externals become so prominent that internal virtues and vices are not treated at all.[2]

We may, in fact, have the wrong emphasis altogether with these externals. Or else why do our non-dancing daughters get pregnant out of wedlock? And why do our rigid fellows who will not drink or smoke, not seem to care whether they get a girl in trouble? And why, most devastating of all, have so many who were brought up in the strict negativism of the fundamentalists turned their backs on the gospel, shedding first all these restrictions and later the heart of the message? Why, in short, have they failed to find grace in the midst of legalistic rigidity?

> New occasions teach new duties; time makes ancient good uncouth;
> They must upward still, and onward, who would keep abreast of Truth:
> Lo, before us gleam her camp-fires! we ourselves must Pilgrims be,
> Launch our Mayflower, and steer boldly through the desperate winter sea,
> Nor attempt the Future's portal with the Past's blood-rusted key.[3]

The rigid attitude which bucks any change as an evil wind that blows ill, must also reckon with the words of Jesus to another mind-set mentality: "Nor do people put new wine into old wineskins—otherwise the skins burst, the wine is spilled and the skins are ruined. But they put new wine into new skins and both are preserved."[4] The old wineskins of our tradition must crack and spill out that good news which is always fresh and invigorating. And which, unquestionably, refuses to remain in any nineteenth-century patterns.

NOTES:

1. See Matt. 7:8,9.
2. Carl F. H. Henry, *Christian Personal Ethics* (Grand Rapids: Wm. B. Eerdmans Publishing Company, 1957), pp. 422, 425, 426.
3. James Russell Lowell, "The Present Crisis."
4. Matt. 9:17 (Phillips).

10.

Familiarity Breeds Contempt

DR. George M. Docherty of Washington, D.C., tells of a youth service in which he attempted to instruct young people about the worship service. The group included youths from church families and young people who had hardly any relationship with the church. They were dubbed "the untouchables."

"To our surprise the untouchables were far more appreciative of the meaning of the beauty of holiness we were seeking to bring to them than the children for whom both the Church School and Sunday worship had already become a custom. The difficult teenagers at the service (those who talked or giggled) were almost always from the churchy homes."[1]

Why is it that in many churches there is general whispering, talking, and widespread unrest prior to the service? Why is it that the organ prelude is played over a background of continual chatter which utterly disregards anything that might call the congregation to worship? Why, too, is there a rising hubbub during the offering, and when the service concludes, why does the congregation exit amid laughter and noise? Has anything really happened in the service that might be called an experience of worship?

We have lost respect for the holy. We come to church so regularly that we act as if we own the place. (And perhaps we did help to pay for it.) The building and the sanctuary are so familiar to us that the thoughts of holiness or the presence of God hardly cross our minds. We listen to the same old choir and we can usually tell what the preacher is going to say before he says it. This is our church and any stranger walking in would know that we were meeting our friends here, but would hardly think that any of us were expecting to meet God.

In losing the idea of the sacred, we have forgotten that Moses removed his shoes at the place where God met him. His reaction was one of awe. I'm not suggesting adopting this custom (as some Christians have), but I am asking why we so seldom think about the possibility of a spiritual experience? We call our churches sanctuaries—consecrated, holy places where mortal men may enter the presence of the Eternal. Every church can be a holy place, unless we desecrate it by our familiarity.

The four-year-old boy sat between his grandmother and father through a worship service. The service had opened with the singing of "Peace, Be Still." Afterwards his grandmother complimented him for being so quiet. He answered: "Didn't you hear them singing, please be still?"

Unlike this small boy, our familiarity with worship makes our singing of the hymns a mere mouthing of familiar (and sometimes unfamiliar) music, which we sing only because we happen to be in church. We probably don't sing outside of church, except for humming some TV commercial. The Scripture which is read without enthusiasm we receive as a matter of fact. Many never consider it as God's word for the moment —powerful, meaningful, charged with the possibility of changing our lives. From the title in the bulletin we have doped out what the sermon is going to be about, and if there happens to be a joke we laugh. That joke may be all we remember from the message. The prayers and all the rest of it hang about our necks like millstones as we settle down in our complacent familiarity.

David Head has suggested that some of us sound like this in church: "Almighty God, there are so many uncertain factors in life. We pray that we may be a little more certain of You. We ask You to be good to us sometimes, to bless us now and again, to give us in some small way an occasional release from our doubts and worries. We believe there are times, even if not frequent, when we deserve Your blessing. Do not let us down. Amen."[2]

One Sunday while his service was being telecast, the minister was amazed at the electrifying effect it had on his congregation. Nobody yawned, nobody nodded during the sermon, everybody sang out on the hymns and every head remained bowed during prayer. The cameras were on!

Why don't we behave that way every Sunday? Where are the alert Christians who refuse to take everything for granted and who want to *meet God* in this most vital hour of the week—not just give Him the nod? Where, indeed, are the Christians who will worship on holy ground?

Most of us are not alert or expectant of anything. If anyone should remotely suggest that here there *could* be an experience of the living God, we would look very surprised and answer: "Nothing like that ever happens in our church! I know. I've been here for years. You can't tell me that anything takes place on Sunday morning at eleven. We just come to church, that's all."

Part of our lack of expectancy is the fault of the minister. How can anything ever be expected to happen if the words from the pulpit are always the same, and truth is expressed without any imagination? And yet the circle comes back to us in the pew again—how can life ever be touched by God's Spirit in the present unless an air of expectancy hangs over the congregation?

A speaker was introduced at a women's club with these words: "This is Professor — one of the great thinkers of our time. He will think for us today!" Many Christians expect their minister to do their thinking for them. Indeed a minister may realize that people want something easy to digest and not too hard to swallow. It must be served up in the lightest, airiest fashion so that no one will have to chew hard. It must also contain the old familiar words. Otherwise some will think something is wrong with the minister's theology. So the temptation for many a minister is to preach that which the congregation wants to hear and to throw in those familiar words which set up acceptable reflex actions. All of which makes a fresh experience of God in worship well nigh impossible.

Nothing will ever happen if we only expect the same old stuff. Because that is all we will hear. And we will walk out again mumbling to ourselves: "That was the same old stuff. Just another sermon. Didn't mean much to me." To ourselves we say this, but to everybody else we say that it sure was a good gospel message, just right for those sinners who came this morning. We enjoyed it, too.

We enjoyed it? Why don't we tell the truth? Or do we really think this shallow familiar repetition is all there is to worship?

If we are looking for the faith mother had or the old-time religion, we are probably in search of the sentimental, not God. What we have is a hankering for the familiar rather than a willingness to shove off into the adventure of encounter. A sentimental lady once called out to Jesus during his message: "Oh, what a blessing for a woman to have brought you into the world and nursed you."[3] Or, in other words, "Your mother must be proud of you; you're such a good boy." She felt a shiver go up and down her spine as Jesus talked. It was all so pious and good! But religion is more than sentiment. Jesus did not let the woman stay in her sentimental mood. "A far greater blessing," he said, "to hear the word of God and obey it." Not sentiment but the ear open to hear God speak, and a life changed by obedience to that word.

We have not heard the word of Jesus, however. Familiarity has so dulled us in our churches that the violent encounters which we read about in Scripture and in church history do not occur any longer. When Isaiah went to the temple at a crisis time in his people's history, he had such a vision of God that he never forgot it. There in that place, which in all probability was familiar to him, he "saw the Lord high and lifted up, and his train filled the temple."[4] *Anything* can happen when we come to the house of God in expectation and faith.

The bulletin of one worship service carried a slight misprint in one of the hymns. It may yet prove to be appropriate and should perhaps be sung in this new version: "*W*ise up, O Men of God."

NOTES:

1. George M. Docherty, *One Way of Living* (New York: Harper & Row, Inc., 1958), p. 98.
2. David Head, *He Sent Leanness* (New York: The Macmillan Company, 1962), p. 25.
3. Luke 11:27 (Phillips).
4. Isa. 6:1.

11.
"Playing Church"

ANY minister who would get up on a Sunday and ask his congregation how many had brought one person to the church during the last year would receive a pitiful response. Even some of the most active laymen never consider it a necessity to bring people to church with them. They may go along for years without bringing one other person—that is, a non-churchgoer or a so-called heathen, of whom there are a few left.

It is not that Christians are unconcerned about these neighbors of theirs. They are very much concerned and they may even occasionally pray for them. They are convicted they ought to do something, but when it comes right down to it they don't do anything. As a result the churches continue in the same rut they have always been in, and new members join only because they've been looking for a church and are already convinced anyway. Perhaps they think it's about time their children had a little Christian instruction in Sunday school. From my experience few new members come because of the endeavors of Mr. Average Christian.

The Synod of Southern California of the United Presbyterian Church, United States of America, reported that in 1968 the more than 250 churches showed a membership of 188,000.

I choose this example since a progressive church in Southern California finds itself in a rapidly exploding area.

The church lost during that year almost 2500 members. What was happening? Were these 188,000 Christians evangelizing, sharing the good news? What were they doing?

Probably playing church. They wouldn't call it that, of course. They were busy teaching Sunday school or singing in the choir, ushering or serving on committees. But when it came to visiting new prospects, Mr. Average Christian did not have time. He was too much involved in the activities of the church (and sometimes, of course, he was just too busy for any church activities at all), that he always had an excuse.

Dr. Masao Takenaka of Japan is quite correct when he defines *our* concept of evangelism as "the lifting of fish out of a dirty river called the world, and placing them in a clean pool called the Church." As if that is supposed to be the task of Christians. Because what happens is that most Christians are content to swim around in that clean pool, while they forget all about that dirty river. (Besides, the pool isn't that clean!)

Nowhere in the words of Jesus can we find any encouragement for playing church, for merely keeping the wheels spinning within the organization. This whole concept is foreign to Biblical Christianity: "Go ye into all the world and preach. . . ."[1] Jesus did not say for us to go into all the churches. The thrust of Christianity is outward. When we turn it inward, we begin to substitute activity for action and introspection for involvement.

Actor Reginald Gardner tells the amusing story of a Hollywood producer who attempted to surpass his brother. His brother had given a brand-new Cadillac to his mother for her birthday. The Hollywood producer bought a mynah bird for $10,000. The bird spoke eleven languages and sang grand opera. On the night of her birthday he called her long distance and asked: "What did you think of the bird, Mama?" "Delicious!" she replied.

Have we misused the good news of God in such an atrocious manner? Devouring God's gifts for ourselves instead of sharing them? Eugene Carson Blake said that the greatest danger of the Church is allowing the organization to obstruct the goals; when we do that we cease to be an instrument of God. Elton Trueblood is even stronger: "Any group that ceases to grow and spread a cause is already dead."

An army must keep its camp clean, be properly equipped and train its men, but its reason for being is *action*. Salesmen must study and know their stuff, but they are not salesmen unless they sell. They cannot attend lectures once a week and then expect the lecturer to do their selling for them! An army that merely cleans up camp or salesmen only content to listen are unheard of. The Church is not simply an organization. It must be an organ used of God in our world. The former president of United States Steel, Clifford Hood, declared: "The Christian Church has a superior quality in its product and every human being is a potential customer." Playing church?

The reason why Presbyterians lost members in Southern California in 1968 was the high mortality rate in the churches. Although 15,500 entered the front doors, many others sneaked out the back. Fifty-five hundred transferred their memberships, over 1000 died, and almost 10,600 were taken off membership rolls. More were removed as delinquents than transferred or died, but even that is deceptive. Few ministers keep an accurate roll anyway, and no minister I know would be guilty of overcutting his membership. I was faced with that question myself, and even though I always pared my rolls, when in doubt I never removed a member. I tended to be quite lenient in that department. Since most of us would like to make a good showing we do not want to cut ourselves down numerically. Perhaps for every stricken member another delinquent remains on the rolls, making the true mortality rate much higher.

What in the world has happened to those who affirm their faith and then are lost out the back door so soon? Is it really their own fault? Are they all that shallow? Or have the old-timers of the church failed to receive them with open arms? Sad to say there are so many cliques who have closed their doors to newcomers, that the average minister is sick at night because he cannot seem to find in the established groups any room for those new Christians.

The organization for "just us folks" who have been pals over the years allows no one to join this "Christian fellowship." They are a Sunday school class or couples group from way back when, and if any new person joins them, it is a miracle. Many more who come into the church itself are cold-shouldered away. "We will accept you as our friends because you joined the church, but no one is quite like our old-time Christian friends." And who wants to be tolerated like this for long?

Leaders of Good News Clubs for children learn a song which substitutes the word "club" for "heart" and goes like this:

> Into our Club, into our Club,
> Come into our Club, Lord Jesus;
> Be here in Power to bless this hour.
> Come into our Club, Lord Jesus.

Too many Christian adults are still singing this ditty.

What is this deadly nonsense that proclaims from the pulpit that all are welcome and then slams the door on anyone who tries to find a place within that fellowship? Why is it necessary to bypass the old group to form new ones for new members? Why are there duplicate Sunday school classes in some churches revolving around some super-star teacher and a closed shop of learners?

If a former psychotic like Mary Magdalene, a greedy "Communist" like Zaccheus or even a calloused-handed fisherman like Peter would want to join some of our evangelical churches, would they be accepted? Why has the convert from alcoholism, prostitution, gambling, or the one with a former jail sentence such difficulty being accepted in churches? Is the Church *open?*

A family which had just moved into a new neighborhood was anxious to make a good impression. The neighbors seemed cold and made no overture of welcome. One day her youngest son ran in and announced, "Mommy, the lady down the street asked my name today!"

His mother was overjoyed: "How nice. And then what did she do?"

"Then she gave it to the policeman," the boy said.

Can it be that we are similarly aloof? The club atmosphere is poison. But it occurs with such monotonous regularity that anyone who comes near such a church can smell it a mile away. No wonder that when they do come in, they go bounding out the back door faster than they came in the front.

When Norman Price, a writer for the *London Sunday Pictorial,* was seriously searching for God, he first consulted the experts. He wrote to a half dozen bishops and found them evasive. He went to church, but the disinterest with which he was confronted brought him to cynicism and despair. Now he concludes that only man's love is eternal and can make the world safe for generations to come. He downgrades organized religion because of his unhappy experiences with Christians. That kind of story can be repeated—to our shame—a thousand times.

"I will never refuse anyone who comes to Me,"[2] said Jesus. If we really believe him, we cannot help but put it into practice. A closed fellowship is a travesty on our faith. It is "playing church" in the very worst way. Besides, if we don't stop playing in what we think to be a clean pool, how can we ever become sensitive to that dirty river which just keeps rolling along?

NOTES:

1. Mark 16:15.
2. John 6:37 (Phillips).

12.

"Goody-Goodies"

LUCY and Linus stand hand in hand with big smiles on their faces and tell Charlie Brown: "We're brother and sister and we love each other."

Charlie knows them and he won't stand for it: "You're hypocrites, that's what you are!" And then he adds: "Do you really think you can fool Santa Claus this way?"

"Why not?" replies Lucy. "We're a couple of sharp kids and he's just an old man."

In the final picture Charlie bows his head against a tree and laments: "I weep for this generation."

Are we sharp conservatives who think we can fool God? One group of people with whom Jesus had the most difficult time was that religious group called the Pharisees. They were religious leaders who were strict in their rites and observances, conservatives who kept to the letter of the law. We still speak of Pharisaism today, a self-righteous temper which subtly enthrones self in the holy place while appearing very religious on the outside. Pharisaism becomes a prostitution of the good, a masquerade of wickedness under the guise of piousness.

There is no better description of Pharisaism than the words of Jesus: "You are like white-washed tombs, which look fine on the outside but inside are full of dead men's bones and all kinds of rottenness. For you appear like good men on the outside—but inside you are a mass of pretence and wickedness."[1] And how can we ever forget Jesus' picture of the Pharisee who entered the temple to address God but wound up only talking with himself? And why? Because he was confident of his own goodness and looked down on others.[2] Jesus is merciless in his condemnation of religious fakery.

Our tendency is to preach about self-righteousness but never to apply it to ourselves. We always think it's for the other fellow when the New Testament describes a religious person like this. Has it anything to say to us? "You . . . think all is well between yourselves and God . . . ; you brag that you are His special friends. Yes, you know what he wants; you know right from wrong and favor the right because you have been taught His laws from earliest youth. You are so sure of the way to God that you could point it out to a blind man."[3]

The people Jesus was speaking to were religious as we think ourselves religious. They considered themselves saved as many of us do in Christianity. They read their Bibles, prayed, fasted, tithed (how many in Christianity actually give ten percent?) and they worshiped God regularly. God could count on them in his world. They were his chosen favorites, the true believers; all the others were irresponsible. They were the good, solid religious people and it never crossed their minds (as it has never crossed the minds of some Christians) that they might not be saved. All their outward religion did not make them any better persons. With all their prayers they were not getting through to God. Though they congratulated themselves on their religious achievements, all they accomplished was to become goody-goodies with a bad smell.

Some forms of religion (Christianity) can make a person proud and selfish (never genuine Christianity, of course). We have all met self-righteous prigs who were so obnoxious that no one but their own kind ever got close to them. Their religion did not make them better, it actually made them worse. No one could tell them anything. They knew it all and they were "in the will of God." But even in us "ordinary" Christians, why is there so little humility? "Everyone that is proud in heart is an abomination to the Lord," in spite of the fact that he mouths orthodox doctrines.[4]

With penetrating insight that mystic William Law has said to us Christians, "No people have more occasion to be afraid of the approaches of pride, than those who have made some advances in a pious life: for pride can grow as well upon our virtues as our vices. . . . Every good thought that we have, every good action that we do, lays us open to pride."[5]

Are religious people aware of these dangers? Many find Christians are indeed sensitive to their sins, but other religious people feel superior because of their religion. Is exclusiveness the problem? Did the Jews feel so exclusive because they alone worshiped the true God? Do Christians feel so superior because Jesus Christ is the answer? That he is the Truth and offers salvation is not in question. But how do we receive that truth? What does the truth do to us? What does it make of us?

As long as anyone remains the center of his own world, everything (including religion) will be *used* by him to minister to him, serve him, satisfy his sense of dominion. Virtue makes him feel more virtuous and prayer makes him feel more spiritual. Doing things for other people produces warmth within, and a substantial contribution to his church causes his chest to swell. Everything becomes fuel for personal ambition, even when he believes himself to be acting on God's behalf. Altogether he may only be making himself into a religious goody-goody.

This is what theologians have always called the original sin of pride—pride which leads to every other vice, and through which the devil became the devil. Through pride we disconnect ourselves from God inwardly, even though we may appear to worship outwardly.

C. S. Lewis writes: "As long as you are proud you cannot know God. A proud man is always looking down on things and people: and, of course, as long as you are looking down, you cannot see something that is above you." Mr. Lewis then raises the probing question of how proud people can possibly affirm their belief in God and be religious. "They are worshipping an imaginary God. They theoretically admit themselves to be nothing in the presence of this phantom God, but are really all the time imagining how He approves of them and thinks them far better than ordinary people."[6]

Lewis offers us a spiritual test: "Whenever we find that our religious life is making us feel that we are good—above all, that we are better than someone else—I think we may be sure that we are being acted on, not by God, but by the devil. The real test of being in the presence of God is that you either forget about yourself altogether or see yourself as a small, dirty object. It is better to forget about yourself altogether."[7]

So, as Lewis says, "the worst of all vices can smuggle itself into our . . . religious life," our very being. Even Christians are not immune. They are in point of fact the prime targets. If Jesus were among us today he would not spare the Christian Church any more than he spared the Jewish synagogue in that first century. He would not overlook our credits, commending us for that which may be good in Protestantism, but neither would he neglect to point out that selfishness which makes so many Christians act smug and superior. And looking down on other people as sinners is no credit to us. Yes, particularly looking down on the ethical man who lives next door because he "does not have the spiritual knowledge" we possess; we are in the kingdom and he is out! When we think like this about in and out, how easy it is for that devilish pride to seep in!

Of course there are those who are in the kingdom and those who are outside. No question about that. Jesus once said to a man: "You are not far from the kingdom of God."[8] Well, good—not far, but not yet in. He was still outside. On the other hand, "Blessed are the poor in spirit, for theirs *is* the kingdom of heaven."[9] Evidently they are in.

But how did they get in? How did we get in? By our own merits? By our goodness and accomplishments? Have we achieved our entrance through our works? Evengelical Christians answer these questions with a resounding "No." And therein lies our hope. "By grace are ye saved through faith; and that not of yourselves: it is the gift of God."[10] Since salvation is received and not achieved, since it is a gift and not worked for, what have we to be proud of then? How can we feel so superior? What gives us the right to look down on any other human being when we are in the lowest, neediest place ourselves? From where do we get the right to be proud when only by humility we have been received by God?

Perhaps a religious goody-goody has never grasped the meaning and implications of the good news. These can only fill us when we turn from our proud selves. Only through a continual denial of self can we make any progress in the Christian life.

C. S. Lewis's words make the point very clear. "I wish I had got a bit further with humility myself. If I had, I could probably tell you more about . . . getting rid of the false self. . . . If anyone would like to acquire humility, I can, I think, tell him the first step. The first step is to realise that one is proud. And a biggish step, too. At least, nothing whatever can be done before it. If you think you are not conceited, it means you are very conceited indeed."[11]

Christians (of all people) should have no trouble taking that step when they simply consider how it was they happened to become Christians in the first place!

NOTES:

1. Matt. 23:27,28 (Phillips).
2. Luke 18:9–14 (Phillips).
3. Rom. 2:17–19, *Living Letters,* Kenneth N. Taylor (Wheaton, Ill.: Tyndale House Publishers, 1962).
4. Prov. 16:5.
5. William Law, *A Serious Call to a Devout and Holy Life.*
6. C. S. Lewis, *Mere Christianity* (New York: The Macmillan Company, 1958), p. 96.
7. *Ibid.,* p. 96–97.
8. Mark 12:34 (Phillips).
9. Matt. 5:3.
10. Eph. 2:8.
11. Lewis, *Mere Christianity,* p. 99.

13. Hypocrites

CHARLIE Brown stands up in a church pew as he looks around at the people. He turns to his friend and asks: "Where are all the hypocrites? I always thought the church was full of hypocrites?"

Many of us have the same reaction as Charlie Brown. We come to church Sunday after Sunday to put on the big show. We get all spruced up, decked out in our Sunday best, and with cocky step march off to church like big shots. Now we are going to shine. When we get there we greet everyone with a happy handshake because we are so friendly. "How are you today? Nice to see you." We put on the big smile and show our teeth because we want people to know that we are happy. (The more we show our teeth the more joy we have in our hearts.) We sit down in our pew feeling very satisfied, and look around over all the other people. "Where are the hypocrites?" we wonder.

Whenever the collection plate is passed we are glad to contribute. Not everyone knows how much we give, but we surely let it be known that we tithe. We are the pillars of the church. Some of us may be called on to pray. No matter, we are always ready with a flow of pious phrases. We know what to say and how to proceed with God in prayer. When we have prayed, we feel even better inside.

We sacrifice, too. We don't frequent shows too often, and we give up certain pleasures to attend church meetings. We make sure that others hear all about this, for we talk freely of God's plan for our lives. We know we live under his guidance and we know exactly what he wants of us. And sometimes (we can't always see this about ourselves) we get just a little bit proud about knowing the mysterious will of God.

The big religious show. But in the heart, the big sin.

Now I don't suspect every smiling, hand-shaking, friendly Christian, because we need more *genuine* Christians who smile and are friendly. But we need the real thing. Nothing faked. Not a type of Hollywood Christianity—the big build up with the terrible letdown. Not what Jesus called the hypocrisy of religious people.

A hypocrite is an actor. He plays a part. He is not really the person he portrays, any more than an actor is the character he represents on stage. The part is something outside of one's true self. There is nothing wrong with friendliness, prayer, sacrifice or giving. But when these become acts of hypocrisy, as mere outward performances, then there is nothing right about them either.

Why do we do some of these things? Behind certain religious acts is a desire to impress. When we appear to be religious in front of people, we are paid for it in compliments and admiration. But if we are paid *here*, can we expect to be paid again *there?* "Verily I say unto you," said Jesus, "They have their reward."[1] If we have our praise now, we will not receive any more when we stand before God in the future hour of accounting. So Jesus takes away from religious people even that goodness, those good works, those prayers and sacrifices—because of their hypocrisy! Why? Because they are not really part of them. Such people are just going through religious motions. They're playing a role.

Here is the quickest way to lose all your Christian works. Simply do them for men to see, for comments of praise. And all those toothy smiles, all those fake handshakes, all those rattled-off prayers, all those tithes, and all that glib talk about knowing God's will are washed down the drain. What a shame! Because you did work so hard for it. And you really did make some sacrifices to be religious.

The excuse most often heard from people who won't enter a church is this: "There are hypocrites in the church." Of course we may answer that the excuse may really be a defense mechanism, but is this enough of a reply? Neither will it do to answer: "Well, come on in then and join us. There's always room for one more." It will be far more advantageous for us to examine our Christian lives, discover the truth in this stock charge, and begin to change.

Let us ask ourselves whether we maintain a double standard in Christianity? Are we far too easily satisfied with ourselves. Is our faith a mere outward performance of certain duties without a corresponding change of heart? Is there "a new creation" whenever a man becomes a Christian? Can the difference in his life be measured—a difference not merely in outer religious acts but in inner attitudes? Has a new behavior pattern come into being? Are new motives through the Spirit of God producing "love, joy, peace, patience, kindness, generosity, fidelity, tolerance and self-control"?[2]

A Christian must be known by his life, not by those religious rites which won't make him much better. Before he goes through all these acts to bolster his faith, he needs an inner transformation. Without that change even religious acts have no value. Therefore Jesus sharply criticizes religious do-gooders.

Perhaps we have been going about it the wrong way. Washing the outside of the cup is comparatively easy, but it is the inside that really counts. And why clean the outside of the cup while the old coffee ring is still there around the inside?

Helmut Thielicke gives us an example of refined hypocrisy which is the result of becoming a spectator of one's own piety. A person may give a Christian testimony, which is naturally an admirable thing. Should we not all be able to testify to what Christ has done for us? Would it be possible to tell how for years we were without him and now have found peace? Many people have been converted through such testimonies. Even the apostles did not tire of sharing their experiences.

> But yet there is always this fact that we can observe in ourselves and in others. In many of these testimonies, especially when they take the form of constantly repeated stories of conversion, a record player over and over again, the focus somehow gets shifted. . . . We really mean in all this to give praise to our Lord, but in reality it has become a bit of autobiographical pomposity. We make an impression with it, and this pleases us; so we go on repeating it frequently. But everything that contributes to the glory of the person and hence takes the glory away from God becomes a lie. . . .
>
> This is exactly what Jesus meant, exactly what one might call the double-tracked, self-contradictory character of our life. True, we worship God by means of our words, we give testimony. But in reality we have already falsified the theme, because we talk about ourselves. . . . Therefore every Christian who wants to confess his Lord . . . must again and again enter into solitude with God, into the quietness of prayer, where no man listens to what is said. . . . How many people there are who do not find God because they are this kind of hypocrite, because this false note . . . creeps into their search for *God!*[3]

It is so easy to put on a Christian performance and never point the finger at ourselves. If there are hypocrites in the churches it must be those others—not us. Yet we cannot change the others, so let us admit the possibility that perhaps we may need to be changed at a point or two. There is one (and only one) whom by the grace of God we can do something about. And if we are willing to examine both our boastful deeds and our inner motivations, we may be on the road to recovery.

There is a story about a bishop who advised a politician to go out into the rain and lift his head toward heaven. "It will bring a revelation to you," he said.

The next day the politician reported: "I followed your advice and no revelation came. The water poured down my neck, and I felt like a fool."

"Well," replied the bishop, "isn't that quite a revelation for the first try?"

NOTES:

1. Matt. 6:3.
2. Gal. 5:22,23 (Phillips).
3. Helmut Thielicke, *Life Can Begin Again* (Philadelphia: Fortress Press, 1963), pp. 117,118.

14. Legalists

"THE many Grace Bible Institutes of Protestantism are not really schools of grace but of legalism," said a fine pastor to me. He went on to describe these schools as emphasizing a list of works. According to him we are very legalistic in evangelical circles, so much so that we lose the very meaning of the love of God.

It is strange that with all our emphasis on the grace of God (which means God's free love toward men who never merit such love) we place demands upon Christians to shape up and do those things which are required in the Bible. (Of course everything has a Biblical base.) But why are there so many legalistic prescriptions for the only way to live? After a Christian has been brought into the wide open spaces of a newly found freedom in Christ, why should he be led back into the jungle of legality, where he has to hack his way through constant undergrowth?

"Keep up your devotions. Establish the habit." Unless a Christian continues with these habits, he is not considered a *good* Christian. He must be able to jump out of bed earlier than the other fellow, get on his knees to pray and read his Bible before he can brush his teeth. We lay down the rule, "No Bible, no breakfast." And it's not a bad one at that, since far too many Christians skip a devotional life or lift a hurried prayer after an evening of TV. But should those who keep it make it into a law?

Decision cards for youth camps list many categories including devotions. Youngsters are urged to sign up. Perhaps it is right to make such decisions, but how many young people have made and broken them before two months passed? And how many more have broken such decisions after years of plodding along, with subsequent guilt feelings? Very real and very deep guilt feelings: "I can't be the Christian I'm supposed to be. I don't measure up. I can't keep up these habits. I'm not a good Christian."

There is placed upon the Christian also the responsibility to witness. He staggers under the weight of this compulsion to tell everyone he meets. He had better testify if he wishes to qualify as a good Christian.

And so develops the strained situation of the zealous Christian who attempts to speak to a brassy businessman on the train.[1] The businessman sits there sucking on his cigar and pays no attention to the fidgety Christian in the next seat. The Christian is under such tension to say something, that he finally breaks out with: "May I tell you about the most important thing in the world?" Which is not a bad beginning at that.

The tycoon takes another puff on his cigar, settles back in his seat and then cuts him down: "Well, son, if it's insurance —I've got enough. If it's oil wells, I don't touch them. And if it's religion—I'm saved." At the next stop a moody Christian gets off the train having failed once more to live up to his calling. He has failed to add another star to his crown.

And then there is that bit of teaching straight out of the law that Christians should be separated. "Come out from among them, and be ye separate, saith the Lord."[2] That is Scripture. But there are Christians who take this so legally that they separate themselves from every form of *life*. They attempt to go out of the world altogether, as if they were already in heaven. To them it means a few rules not only to live by but most of all by which to cut off contact with the world. "What fellowship has righteousness with unrighteousness? And what communion has light with darkness?"[3] But what they are doing is erecting walls which alienate them from the world and allow them to squeeze out from under any involvement with sinners. And all the while they hide in their own circles.

The most obvious example is found among the Amish community. The Amish are totally apart from the world. But even their own small group splinters to divide again and again. Nevertheless, it is not necessary to search for illustrations of separationism this far out. Many evangelicals really believe that they have been fished out of the dirty world into the clean pool of the Church.

But what kind of Christianity is this which refuses to follow Jesus into the world? Jesus ate with sinners, forgave an adulteress who should have been stoned according to the law, and touched outcast lepers. For all of this he was looked down upon by the separationists of his day and considered "worldly." The difference was that Jesus was separated (if we must use this word) in his heart. He did not separate himself from people. His separation was an inner one, whereas ours is too often outward.

Through such maneuvers Christians have stepped right back into legalities without actually living in the freedom that is found in Christ. And in our attempt to live by rules and regulations, we have only made salvation a piece of justifying legislation. "So many laws argues so many sins."[4]

Why do we never hear in this legalistic claptrap the fact that we are *not able to keep any of our decisions?* It is not within our power, no matter how eagerly we may try to live the Christian life successfully. We are not self-sufficient. We have gradually moved out of the realm of grace—which means we have entered the field of works: "We can keep our own decisions, if only we make the right ones." No, we cannot. Not even Christian decisions. We are always dependent on God. The more we make and break decisions, the worse guilt feelings we incur. Christianity is not a legalistic carrying out of Christian duties, but it should become a daily, personal relationship with our heavenly Father.

So it goes in every area of Christian activity, like going to church, attending meetings, being seen in Christian circles. *Of course* Christian fellowship is necessary for our growth! Yet how many attend these meetings with wooden regularity out of a sense of duty? They feel compelled to do these things, or else . . . Or else what? Why this sense of obligation, this burden one carries around on one's back? Is this the freedom of which Jesus speaks: "You shall know the truth and the truth shall make you free?"[5] What freedom is there in a stolid carrying out of one's Christian duties?

It seems that instead of knowing God as our Father who accepts us as his children, Christians are always talking about "the Lord." This very language intensifies the nature of law, for the Lord must be obeyed. He must be served and his will done. We must measure up to his demands. Thus the picture of the Judge looms over young sensitive spirits; one young man brought up in this tradition felt so guilty about something one week, that the next week he doubled his tithe to the church. He obviously had no idea of the freedom Christ speaks about, even though he was brought up in a church which fervently believes itself to be preaching the gospel.

If God is our Father we will begin to think differently. A father will indeed punish, but his correction proceeds from his love. A father will be strict and make demands, but only out of his inner concern. Most important, a relationship has been established when God is truly our Father and we are his children. Can we begin to think of that relationship, rather than a static fulfilling of the will of the Lord?

Surely Jesus taught this. The word most frequently on his lips is not "Spirit," or "God," and never "The Almighty," but always "Father." It may be that with all our legalism we are floating on the surface of life, failing to explore the depths of our faith. We attempt to please God without ever examining ourselves, and our real sins remain buried under the layers of church attendance, witnessing, devotions and separationism which we spray over them regularly.

If at any time there does arise to our consciousness something from our subconscious which is rather nasty or evil or resentful, we say to ourselves: "But that's not the real me. I must be dreaming. I'm not like that." Whatever I happen to like about myself I accept, and whatever I happen not to like about myself I dismiss. It is an inescapable fact that we do not want to see ourselves as we really are, since honesty is so painful. But this dark other-self with all its faults and sinful defects is *also* me.

The good news tells me that I am accepted by God and set free through Jesus Christ. This means that God does not only accept my good self (whatever that is!) but my bad self—in other words, my total self. Therefore I do not have to cover my evils legally, since God receives me as I am. If all this is true, it should not be too painful to begin an honest self-examination, instead of retreating from ourselves into a shell of regulations.

When the New Testament says that we should "grow in grace,"[6] it evidently means that this is a Christian necessity. We are not told to grow in laws and demands, or to make more decisions, but simply to mature in the grace of God. That is, to know that we are really loved by God in spite of all our sinful frailties. Since far too many Christians are growing in law rather than in grace, these words ought to be taken seriously by us all, before we lose the next generation through our own stupidity.

NOTES:

1. Thorton Wilder, *Heaven's My Destination.*
2. II Cor. 6:17.
3. II Cor. 6:14.
4. John Milton.
5. John 8:32.
6. II Pet. 3:18.

15.

And Bigots

A WELL-KNOWN Christian spokesman wrote an article in which he broadly slandered another Christian group. He stated categorically that they did not teach the truth from the Bible and said that they were not saved. He made his point in one sentence, quoting one of their spokesmen. The sentence was composed by wrenching three phrases from two different paragraphs, none of which were originally consecutive and combining these without the customary . . . indicating omissions.

Such a deed ought to be enough of an example of the bigotry sometimes exhibited in fundamental circles where conservatives try to prove the other fellow dead wrong, a lost soul in eternity. "No one else can be saved but us." This article, however, was more than bigotry; it was a falsification of the facts.

The author of the original article (which he had written twenty-five years earlier) replied in a letter to the publisher of the magazine in which this slanderous article appeared. He pointed out that the Christian spokesman had misquoted him. He also stated that in subsequent articles he had refuted these earlier writings. The editor of that Christian magazine refused to print the correction, and even denied the defendant the simple courtesy of printing his letter! What will we call this? We cannot even call it a free press!

Bigotry is an ugly word. We don't like to use it for Christians. But in spite of the fact that Christianity is for the world, the most blatant separatists often make the Bible actually read: "Christ died only for the good conservative Christians —and nobody else." John 3:16 states a world view: "God so loved the world . . . !" We must not narrow it down for just us folks who really know the Lord: "God so loved us Christians."

Bigotry, though, is not limited to the Church I love. I find it present (surprisingly?) among liberals. Many a liberal speaks broadly of loving all mankind but can viciously undercut a conservative Christian brother whom he labels an out-of-date, old-time pietist. This happens too often to be funny and indicates a gaping weakness in those who supposedly love everybody.

Leslie D. Weatherhead, former minister of the City Temple in London, pointed out that spokesmen from most denominations have published criticisms of Billy Graham. Never once has Graham lifted his voice to tell them their theology was bunk. Weatherhead did not deny the right to criticize, but he did deplore the bigotry of liberal theologians: "I would like to say to you and to me this morning that we must always beware lest criticisms become excuses. If the devil can make us create such a smoke-screen out of dislike of Billy Graham's methods or disapproval of his theory that we can hide from God, then, of course, he is happy. . . . How silly it is to miss being cured because we do not like the doctor."[1]

On the other hand consider the obvious bigotry of those extreme fundamentalists who are unable to see any good in anyone else, who are so far to the right that everybody else has to be to their left. Who gave them the authority to set themselves up as judges of everyone else? Harry and Bonaro Overstreet in their book *The Strange Tactics of Extremism* cite examples of those conservatives who denounce other conservatives.

"Wherever issues are drawn between opposing sides there are always those who desire compromise and a middle course. . . . But where one of the sides in the conflict has the eternal truth . . . to compromise in the slightest is to dishonor and destroy the faith." The Overstreets comment that this refusal to compromise is not between evangelicals and Communists. Not even between evangelicals and Christians "commonly called liberal or modern." This is opposition to and refusal to compromise with other theologically conservative and fundamentalist groups who have some doctrinal differences.[2]

But why such bigotry in that solid Christian middle, in that sound committed core of Christianity? Why the need to expose all heresy and maintain the truth in a divisive manner? Why downgrade anyone who graduates from certain seminaries, or belongs to a denomination under suspicion? Why, for example, the *overemphasis* on the doctrine that the whole world is going to hell except those who hear and respond to the gospel? Does not God *love* the world? Or why must a person prove his Christian faith before he can be accepted by the saved? Why does a man have to use the proven clichés before the "in group" even listens?

Without question Christians feel that they are on the right track because they have believed in the "one name under heaven given among men, whereby we must be saved."[3] The name of Jesus, according to that Scripture, is the only name: "Neither is there salvation in any other." If Jesus is the only begotten Son of God and the Savior of *the world,* then there can be no other. Christianity has always proclaimed the uniqueness of Jesus Christ—God become man, crucified for our sins and risen from the dead. Jesus is not in competition with leaders of other religions. He is not simply a leader of a religion. He is the very incarnation of God—God personally entering time and history for man's redemption.

Pascal attested to the uniqueness of the Christian faith when he said: "No other religion than ours has taught that man is born in sin, no sect of philosophers has said so, hence none has told the truth." "I see many religions, contrary to one another, and therefore all false save one . . . I see the Christian religion wherein prophecies are fulfilled; and that is more than everyone can do."[4]

Christians, then, cannot be wishy-washy about truth, just as we cannot be broadminded in other matters. If two times two is four, tolerance will not allow for five. If Julius Caesar was murdered on March 15th, 44 B.C., then he did not die a natural death in 45. If there is one God, there cannot be several. Tolerance is not the question. Therefore, if Christ is the Savior of the world ("neither is there salvation in any other") then one cannot be broadminded about that either. Those who say that religious leaders are all good, imply that not one of them is good in the fullest, truest sense. To make of Jesus simply another teacher among the world's many teachers denies his uniqueness as well as his own words.

It may be true that because of an overemphasis on this point Christians become bigots, but this is a misunderstanding of the truth. A convinced American misunderstands democracy if he goes around shooting all foreigners. An inner conviction need not result in bigotry.

A bigot may be covering his doubts. His loud affirmations may be hiding his deep uncertainties. He may shout: "We have the truth in Christ," but he forgets that Christ does not make bigots out of his followers—this is our own misreading of his message. Yet these strong Christians have a comeback: "Did not Jesus himself throw the moneychangers out of the temple? Did he not condemn the religious leaders as hypocrites? Did he not say, 'he who is not with me is against me?' "[5]

Yes, he did drive the moneychangers out, but that was hardly bigotry. He was disturbed at their misuse of God's house. It was to be a house of prayer, not an institution for economic gain. As for "he who is not with me is against me," he said this to those who openly opposed him. They had just told him that he was not a representative of God but of the devil. Obviously they showed themselves to be antagonistic.

If, because we must defend the faith, we still feel we dare not tolerate others, let Jesus speak to us again: "He that is not against us is on our part."[6] That seems to be a contradiction. But in that situation his disciples condemned some who were working on Jesus' behalf, but who were not of their "in group." They did not belong to the apostolic band. Jesus did not recommend bigotry here!

What do we remember of Jesus? Was he a bigot? Certainly not. He stood up forcefully for that which was right. He spoke truth. He did not tolerate error. If he found hypocrisy, he exposed it. If he discovered faith, he commended it, whether in or out of the established boundaries. And he knew he had come not to condemn the world, but to save it.[7]

The Christian who in spite of his evangelical fervor cannot allow anyone else to have a place in the sun, needs to examine his own position carefully. Why has he become so small? Has Jesus actually called him to be a bigot?

NOTES:

1. Leslie D. Weatherhead, from a sermon preached at the City Temple, London, during the Billy Graham campaign.
2. Harry & Bonaro Overstreet, *The Strange Tactics of Extremism* (New York: W. W. Norton & Company, 1964), p. 149.
3. Acts 4:12.
4. Blaise Pascal, *Pensées,* Section 9, No. 605; Section xi, No. 692.
5. See Matt. 12:30.
6. Mark 9:40.
7. John 3:17.

16.

Anxiety

OURS has been called an age of anxiety. We are on edge, in a hurry to keep up with our full schedules and our superiors' demands, pressured for time, caught up in this fast-paced jet age in which we find ourselves running faster than a lizard on a hot rail. As a result we have experienced an increase in mental illnesses, a growing demand for psychiatric services, and a phenomenal rise in the consumption of drugs and pills. Our mental institutions house millions, and many more barely keep themselves from going over the cliff.

Christians are also caught up in this frenzy. They do not seem able to escape the pressures into quietness to hear the voice of God. They also meet schedules, battle tensions, get anxious, develop neuroses, and are sometimes overcome by inordinate fears. They take pills to calm down and other pills to pep up. They frequent the doctor's office and run to the psychoanalist as well. They are saved, yes, but perhaps they do not seem to be saved from fret, anxiety, melancholy, depression or even mental illness.

What is the answer? Drug manufacturers extol the virtues of new drugs and tranquilizers: "Harassment and worry are replaced by an unfluctuating mood of untroubled composure. Daytime sedation without hypnosis calms the quaking inner self." And some physicians instead of trying to help people cope intelligently with life, prescribe more and more dope. How long can we avoid an honest examination of the self? Christians who continually escape their real problems will only continue with those same hostilities and repressed frustrations.

Motion picture actress Gene Tierney after four years of mental illness had this comment about herself: "My illness was something I was responsible for. It was my own fault, not the fault of anyone else. The trouble was my lack of understanding of what I could cope with and what I couldn't cope with." Few Christians will be that honest about themselves. Even worse, they fail to realize that only such basic honesty will end the nervous breakdowns we heap on ourselves.

One psychiatrist asks which nerves break down? He answers that our nerves do not break down but we ourselves do. We want to have a change of pace. We want to escape. What easier way to get away from a situation than to have a nervous breakdown? Even though it may be unconsciously, he firmly believes we engineer the disaster ourselves.

How much good does it do to tell people from the pulpits to stop worrying and start living? How much value is a sermon against anxiety or neuroses which only recites endless illustrations of how tense life is in our age? (We know this already!) We need to have spelled out for us how to deal with this troublesome life but we hear precious little about this. Instead we are instructed to use the Christian faith for acquiring a kind of cheery charm to cover all those anxieties. Such instruction is a perversion of the good news of God, and does little more than the tranquilizers.

A psychiatrist told a mother who had brought her troubled child in for treatment, "I will see Johnny next month, but you need help yourself. You are upset and worried about him, so I suggest you take one of these tranquilizers each day until I see you again." The next month she brought her son back. "How is Johnny getting along?" asked the psychiatrist. Replied his mother: "Who cares?"

Jesus never avoided problem situations. He went straight to the heart of each one. They were, however, acknowledged to be problems. We cannot begin to cope with the problems in our Christian lives unless we first admit they exist. If an evangelical isn't allowed to have any problems, what kind of nonsense has he been taught? And yet if he can't find any help through his Christian teaching, what good is it to acknowledge that he has problems? What is the route out of this impasse?

Early in my ministry I developed a condition for which I had to enter the hospital. An operation became a necessity because, according to the doctor, this condition had developed through excessive pressures and unusual worries. He was right. As a young minister I felt under the pressure of getting the job done and getting the gospel out to everyone. And I must have worried about it. Therefore it became necessary during the time in the hospital to examine my motives, my worries, and my ministry. Happily the condition has not returned, although that is not to say I am completely free from worry. But I do know how harmful such anxiety can be.

The Christian ought to be willing to deal with these pressures when they exist in his life. At least it does seem that this is what we set out to do in our Christian lives. The band-aid treatment of drugging the mind or controlling the emotions artificially never reaches the deeper disorders within. The message of Christianity can and must reach life at every level; if it fails to accomplish this, the fault does not lie with the gospel but with the individual.

While fears and worries are generally attached to things external like finances, jobs, the family, injury, sickness or death, anxiety centers about the self. It springs from a sense of insecurity and inadequacy. To us anxieties may appear quite reasonable. We have our explanations for them. Otherwise, of course, we would not hold on to them! But if your life is riddled by nerves, what has your faith done for you? If you believe the truth and nurse a nasty ulcer, wouldn't it be well to discover why you developed the ulcer?

Ordinary psychotherapy may clear up many of these problems, and psychological insight may diminish the degree of your neuroses, but complete healing will take more than understanding yourself. The Christian faith offers a complete remedy through a new relationship with God as our Father, Christ our Savior and the Holy Spirit our daily Guide. The potential is so vast that with or without other helps, Christians can be made whole and healed spiritually. This is the *full meaning* of the much used word "salvation." Salvation is the making whole of man, the complete man.

Psychiatrist Fritz Kunkel tells of a woman who had a son in the war. The boy wrote letters home frequently, but suddenly and without warning the letters stopped. She tried to be patient for two weeks and then she became unduly anxious. She could not eat, sleep or work. Her physician did his best to reassure her and gave her a sedative. (Naturally.) Her minister said the same things as the doctor, suggesting self-control and hard work. (Cheery charm.) He also prayed with her. She became even more filled with anxiety and was heading for a nervous breakdown. After several weeks a half-dozen letters arrived all at once. There had been a delay at the front.

She was naturally relieved and thankful—up to a point. Then she began to question: "Why did this happen to me? If this state of suspense had lasted a few days longer I might have collapsed completely. I could have committed suicide because I was convinced he was dead. God is cruel. He played a dirty trick on me. Why did he allow this to happen? I used to believe in God, but not any more. I doubt the whole thing." And then, even worse, she tried to forget that the whole episode had ever taken place.

Many a person with shallow faith has found that his faith failed in the test of circumstances. Then, instead of learning something from the experience or preparing for the next emergency, he has been unable to recover himself or to face his inadequacies. The mother in Fritz Kunkel's story will be no more ready for the next test than she was for the previous one.

It is not possible to mature spiritually and remain immature personally. A Christian must, by the grace of God, be willing to grow out of his unnecessary inhibitions, out of an inferiority complex and all the resultant anxieties. Life comes to us all, testing our capacities, straining our nerves. If we misunderstand these times as cruel, or believe that useless tricks are being played on us, how will we ever cope with life? Perhaps the pressures will be more constant and less dramatic for many, but it is never possible to live joyously with anxiety. Can anyone live happily with fear or be content with a cancer?

Let Christians learn something from the simplicity of faith Jesus teaches. This faith is based on God's love and care for us. "Look at the birds in the sky. They never sow nor reap nor store away in barns, and yet your Heavenly Father feeds them. Aren't you much more valuable to him than they are? Can any of you, however much he worries, make himself an inch taller? . . . So don't worry and don't keep saying, 'What shall we eat, what shall we drink or what shall we wear?' That is what pagans are always looking for; your Heavenly Father knows that you need them all. Set your heart on his kingdom and his goodness, and all these things will come to you as a matter of course.

"Don't worry at all then about tomorrow. Tomorrow can take care of itself! One day's trouble is enough for one day."[1]

NOTES:

1. Matt. 6:26–34, *passim* (Phillips).

17.

Social Concern?

J. S. R. RUSSELL of Mexico City wrote a letter to *Time* magazine: "Sir, You submit that Christianity is resurgent, and thereupon pose the question: 'Is it possible that Christianity is really true, after all?' A thunderous reply in the negative should come from all who can run and read—crime, corruption, delinquency, clash of ideologies—chaos everywhere and church every Sunday—bah!"

A person from outside the Church (Mr. Russell calls himself a pragmatist) may comment on this sad state of affairs in society and therefore find reason to reject Christianity. Churchmen, however, also decry the increase in crime, alcoholism, divorce, sexual laxity and juvenile delinquency, as well as the seeming ineffectualness of the Church. Billy Graham feels that a hundred million American church members living the Christian life and putting Christ's teachings into practice would have a tremendous influence on our society. It would seem that the responsibility of America's future rests squarely on the Church. But why have we shown so little concern till now?

Social concern is almost nonexistent in the evangelical churches. What is the reason for this lack? In a slashing book in which he blames our preoccupation with a false piety, Edward Farley writes:

> Obviously the world is placed in the background as something incidental, not quite deserving to be there, like a small child playing with a toy in some remote corner of a conference room. Those in conference do not mind if he is there so long as he does not get in the way. The world is something Protestant piety tolerates so long as its situations and crises do not mar our pilgrimage to saintliness. Such a Christian is therefore in the peculiar position of being placed by God in a world and in a specific environment that he then tries to ignore or put aside. But if God's Word is God's living will addressed to man in every new situation . . . how dare the Christian ignore those situations for something else?[1]

I would only add that not many Christians are so involved with their own piety, either.

Here and there one hears of those who are involved in changing the world around them, but by and large too many Christians are only interested in converting people and getting them into the Church. I have observed that some evangelicals are *only* interested in getting people to make decisions. Whether these people grow in the Christian life or begin to deal with their problems doesn't matter; they have become converts, Christians. (Numbers?) On the other hand there are Christians who only care about getting new members for the churches. Whether they have made a decision—been converted—is incidental. Neither group, however, is socially concerned about the convert's involvement in society—his "good works."

Surely every aspect is vital to a Christian's growth. A person needs to be born anew, converted from his former ways. He needs to join the church. But what happens then? Should not Christians also express social concern? What do we make of the parallel increase in church attendance and crime? Should not Christians become far more involved in social education and action than they now are? Should they not join those organizations in the community which fight crime, gambling, pornography, drug addiction and a host of other evils? Should they not spearhead movements for the sake of Christ in education, business, politics, and scientific research? Should they not seek to express their faith wherever and however they have been called upon to express it, stemming the tide of evil forces, instead of being content to listen to pretty speeches?

Pierre Berton reports on polls conducted in both Canada and the United States. In a list of a dozen suggested sermon topics the subject, "How can I take religion into my business life?" ranked seventh in Canada and last in the USA, far behind such old standbys as "How can I make prayer more effective?" and "Happier families through religion." "If the Church sees its task to be giving the public what it wants," comments Berton, "then it will continue to ignore the ethics and morals of business and industry. The Church . . . cannot long survive, unless, like its founder, it stirs up the people by making large numbers of them acutely uncomfortable."[2]

Have Christians become concerned about avarice, greed, deceptive advertising, the lust for power? Have they spoken out about the profit motive even in times of war?

A lack of social concern is commented upon by Vance Packard, who contends that status has crept into the Church. Therefore the desire to keep quiet on unpopular issues. If this is true, how can the Church speak to the world when she has herself become status conscious? If upper-class churches look down on lower-class churches and people madly climb from one strata to another to improve their standing, can this be considered Christian?

> While the lower-class religions offer consolation for failure, many (but not all) upper-class churches tend to generate the pleasant feelings that everything within the social system is pretty fine just as it is.
>
> As you go up the social scale, services become less emotional and evangelical, and more intellectualized and restrained. . . .
>
> . . . Christianity in mid-century America shows a sizable gulf between practice and preaching. . . . Should one be worshiping in a setting that makes a mockery of one of the core

values of Christianity: the brotherhood of man? At present, the brotherhood of man is in danger of becoming merely a nice intellectual concept.[3]

The Church can hardly speak out on the love of God if she is knee-deep in the muck of status-seeking.

Our lack of social consciousness is also reflected in the arts. When we turn our back on culture, literature, music, painting, sculpture, poetry, and art, dare we lament the lack of Christian motivation? "To be human is to be scientific, yes, and practical, and rational, and moral, and social, and artistic, but to be human further is to be religious also. And this religious in man is not just another facet of himself, just another side to his nature, just another part of the whole. It is the condition of all the rest and the justification of all the rest. . . . No man is religiously neutral in his knowledge of and his appropriation of reality."[4]

In art we have made a fetish of Sallman's pretty head of Christ and in poetry we express trite thoughts in rhyme. In Christian literature we readily accept mediocrity and in our hymns sentimentality. Why have we not emphasized some of the great art of the past or attempted some twentieth-century realism ourselves? Speaking about literature, and addressing himself to Christian publishers as well as to readers, a Christian professor says: "Evangelicals do not read very much at all, and many of them have never read a good modern secular novel because they do not have very much taste for reading in the first place. . . . They do not realize the spiritual message that there is in a deeper understanding of life and its problems as shown up in a good secular novel."[5]

Dr. Kilby concludes his penetrating critique as he discusses the tragedy of our publishing policy which is too scared to offend the saints: "A policy of giving the public what it wants is an unworthy one whether in Christian or secular things because, however reasonable it appears, it inevitably involves hedging and extenuation, finding it easy to justify anything from pornography in secular publishing to unadulterated sentimentality in religion. Writing and publishing are types of leadership, and leadership involves moral responsibility."

Whether in the political arena, the world of business and finance, education and psychology, research and science, the social world or the cultural milieu, only a vital faith can propel the Christian into an orbit of action. He can no longer hide within the rotating wheels of the Church, nor can the Church herself afford to hide within by talking only to herself. Our Savior who went into the world established a different pattern for us.

Not long ago a meeting took place where a few spoken words took on almost symbolic significance. The meeting involved some of the world's top churchmen, who sat down with the Negro author James Baldwin. They discussed the racial situation. After some time one of the bishops, fingering a cross dangling on his chest from a chain around his neck, pleaded: "Time, gentlemen, this is what we need. We need more time!"

Baldwin leaned forward across the table and snapped: "You can't have it." Then, pointing to the bishop's cross in his fingers, he added: "And the sooner you get that from your chest on to your back, the better it'll be."

NOTES:

1. Edward Farley, *Requiem for a Lost Piety* (Philadelphia: The Westminster Press, 1966), p. 73. Copyright © 1966, W. L. Jenkins. The Westminster Press. Used by permission.
2. Pierre Berton, *The Comfortable Pew* (Philadelphia: J. B. Lippincott Company, 1965), pp. 39, 40.
3. Vance Packard, *The Status Seekers* (New York: David McKay Company, 1959), pp. 201, 206.
4. Henry Zylstra, *Testament of Vision* (Grand Rapids: Wm. B. Eerdmans Publishing Company, 1958), pp. 145, 146.
5. Clyde S. Kilby, "The Artistic Poverty of Evangelicals," *Eternity*, 1965.

18.
The Juice of Prejudice

"When God finished making the world
He had a few stinking scraps of mud left over
and used it to make a yellow dog"
(and when they hate any race or nation
they name that race or nation
in place of the yellow dog).
They say and they say and the juice of prejudice drips from it.
They say and they say and in the strut of fool pride spit in the wind.[1]

Cecil Poole, assistant district attorney of San Francisco, is a Negro. He lives in a white neighborhood. One day his six-year-old daughter came running into the house with a report that must have shocked her father: "There's a cross on our lawn, all burned. Why is it there?" Mr. Poole met the crisis quietly: "Some Christian," he said, "has lost his way."

It may be far from the mark to equate the KKK with Christians. The KKK is abhorred by the whole Christian world except for that tiny minority who have taken the cross of Jesus as the badge of their group. How they can do this is beyond my understanding, and I deem it completely unnecessary to waste space on this enigma.

But Poole was right. Many Christians have lost their way. (Perhaps they had never found it in the first place.) It may be that their acceptance of Christ never changed any of their prejudices. They closed the door to the Spirit of Christ into *that* department of their lives. Billy Graham says he was labeled radical and liberal, even called a Communist, for integrating his evangelistic crusades. He had made up his mind against segregation *before* the court decision of 1954. And who called him these names? Certain groups of conservatives and fundamentalist "brothers."

It is still a sad commentary on Christians that any mention of the race issue precipitates an argument almost at once. It is dangerous to talk about race. Minds are so set and determined that they can only look at the problem in one way. No one desires to change.

And yet, Christians do not want to appear prejudiced either. So they avoid the subject. Some Christians are not so closed minded. They attempt to alleviate racial tensions. Their efforts are admirable. The only trouble is that they are awfully hard to find.

A Japanese consul was invited to a dedication ceremony of a Japanese Christian church in Los Angeles. He agreed to come if the pastor would make an appointment with him. So they made the appointment for the next day. But when the pastor arrived, he found the consul's attitude cold.

"What happened?" asked the minister.

The consul refused to talk about it. After considerable urging, he related this story: "Yesterday, after you called I went to a barber shop. 'We don't shave Orientals here,' said the barber. I asked him why not? He said: 'It would hurt our business.' I questioned him further, but he only said that he didn't want trouble and that he couldn't take me into the shop. By this time a policeman walked in. The other barber had summoned him, and the policeman said: 'I think you'd better go.' I went. And when I shut the door behind me, I shut the door also on all your so-called Christian democracy. I will not take part in that ceremony."

It is beside the point whether the barber was a Christian or not. The story is the same in every sector of the country. An Indian student on a bus with a Christian group became ill. One of the women, who had herself left Hinduism to become a Christian, got off the bus with him to find a temporary lodging for him. She called up a minister of her denomination and explained the situation. She was continuing on the trip, but could the student spend the night there? The minister refused. He gave as his reason that he could not afford to have his neighbors see a dark-skinned man come into his home to spend the night.

At hearing this the student told this Christian woman that she was a traitor to forsake Hinduism for Christianity, and that, when he returned to India he would tell how a caste system was observed in the United States. The minister telephoned back to the bus station and asked that his name be not revealed. Could it have been possible that on the next Sunday he was to preach on the parable of the Good Samaritan—whose only preoccupation was to help someone in need, regardless of race or religion?

Why are Negroes denied entrance into some evangelical seminaries, so that they enter more liberal ones? Why have Negroes been refused by evangelical mission boards, who send white missionaries to Africa? As late as 1964 one such mission board dropped its color bar and of this writing another which specializes in Africa still retains it! It is too crazy to be true—sending missionaries to Africa to convert the Negro and refusing any Negro who wants to go to his own people!

Our whole concept of Christianity is at stake. We may sing this little song in our Sunday schools:

> Jesus loves the little children,
> All the children of the world;
> Red and yellow, black and white,
> All are precious in his sight,
> Jesus loves the little children of the world.

But what happens when we grow up? Do we believe it? Is the good news for the whole world? Are Jew and Greek, bond and free, male and female, and all races of men one in Christ?[2]

Are our castes of sex, religion and race removed by Christ? Did the early Christians break through the wall of prejudice with their preaching and action? Consider that Philip, one of the early Church deacons, led an Ethiopian to Christ in the Gaza strip. And Simon of Cyrene stepped forward to carry the cross of Jesus to the hill of Calvary. What a picture that is for our time!

In Christ all distinctions pass away. And when our Lord says that we are to love our neighbor as ourselves, he adds that "all the law and the prophets hang on this."[3] This is the meaning of the cross. He died for us all. At the foot of the cross there can be no racial barriers. Everyone is Jesus' neighbor. Everyone can become his friend.

In the days following the Civil War an incident took place in a church in Virginia where Negroes had not yet been required to withdraw into their own places of worship. General Robert E. Lee attended, and as the Lord's Supper was about to be celebrated, a Negro went forward to the altar. The white Christians remained in their pews, shocked and resentful. Then Lee himself went forward and knelt beside the man.

We are equal in the sight of God. And when we *leave* the communion table there should be no distinction either. To the contrary, it ought to draw us closer together as we come nearer to Jesus Christ. Have we not read that God has no favorites?[4]

He was working in a day care center. A little boy of four followed him everywhere, attaching himself with what the man thought was admiration. But the boy had just arrived from Israel and had never seen a Negro before. He was really curious, inspecting him at every opportunity. One day the boy touched his own face and then the face of the Negro social worker. Then he spoke a profound truth: "That's just skin."

Christians must make that discovery, too. We have no other choice. We must ask ourselves whether the gospel has accomplished its purpose within us. Has it changed our attitudes? The mass of Christians can be changed if evangelical Christians will set the example. They must break down the walls of prejudice. But if change does not occur, it is doubtful whether the gospel has really reached us!

A Hindu came to a Christian meeting and told the missionary: "You people say you are saved. So am I. As Christ has saved you, so Krishna has saved me."

The missionary in charge answered wisely: "I am very glad to hear that you are saved, very glad. Now we are going down to the outcaste quarters and we are going to see what we can do for these people. Will you join us?"

The Hindu thought it over a moment, and then he said: "Well, sir, I am saved—but I am not saved that far."

How far have *we* been saved? Has it been far enough?

NOTES:

1. Carl Sandburg, *The People Yes,* 51. Copyright, 1936, by Harcourt, Brace & World, Inc. In *Complete Poems* (New York: Harcourt, Brace & World, Inc., 1950), p. 510. Used by permission.
2. See Col. 3:11.
3. Matt. 22:40.
4. See Rom. 2:11 in the *New English Bible, New Testament.*

How to Right the Wrong

"It is better to debate a question without settling it, than to settle it without debate."

—JOUBERT

"The man who is himself conscious of being an individual, and thereby is conscious of his eternal responsibility before God . . . knows, that even if he could with the help of evasions and excuses, get on well in this life, and even if he could have gained the whole world, yet there is still a place in the next world where there is no more evasion than there is shade in the scorching desert."

—KIERKEGAARD[1]

19.
The Need for Confession

IT will now appear obvious that good and bad can be written about Christianity. It all depends from which side of the fence you're looking. (Compare the chapter on "sincerity" in Part One with the chapter on "contentment" in Part Two.)

What lies before us now is the most important task of reconstruction. It is not enough to expose our ills. Anyone can analyze. But how can we right the wrong? How shall we go about the reconstruction?

"Disgraceful," says Lucy to Linus as he hugs his favorite blanket.

"Oh, go away," he says.

"Completely disgraceful," she repeats. "You and that stupid blanket. Are you gonna carry that thing around the rest of your life? When are you going to learn to stand on your own two feet?"

"Waddya mean?" he replies, "I've got just as much will power as anyone else. See? I don't need this blanket! I can throw it away any time I want to. Any time!"

In the next picture they stand there just looking at each other. Linus holds his stomach, his eyes roll and he says, "Good Grief!" He dives for his blanket and hugging it once again exclaims: "I thought I could do it. I actually thought I could do it!" Lucy walks away mumbling: "You're a hopeless case."

Are we a hopeless case? Should we give up in a spirit of despair? Such an attitude will avail us nothing. Yet, on the other hand, we must not be so optimistically foolhardy that we fail to grasp the seriousness of the situation. "I can throw it away anytime!"—but that is followed by the big letdown. What we need is a straightforward, honest examination with an attempt at renewal by the help of God. Our case is not hopeless, but it is mighty sad. The sooner we admit this, the quicker we'll be on our way.

What better place can we begin, then, but with confession—the honest admission of our true state. Jesus came preaching the gospel, "Repent and believe."[2] Change, turn about. This is the message of Christianity to the world. Repentance (change of mind) and faith in the good news that God has personally visited us in Jesus Christ, is that message. But proclaiming it to the world is one thing and listening to it ourselves is another. It is so much easier to tell everyone else to change and never think that we need it also. The time has come to wake up to the facts.

Preaching confession to Christians will hardly be popular. When the prophet Amos first came into Israel after leaving his sheep in the southern kingdom of Judah, he thundered judgment against the nations surrounding Israel. He preached against the sins of Damascus and the transgressions of Gaza. At this his listeners warmed up to him. This man was really proclaiming the word of God—judgment against sinners!

Amos cried out about the betrayals of Tyre and the ruthless acts of Edom—they also would be overthrown by the Lord. The congregation cheered. Now on the edge of their seats, they were with the preacher one hundred percent. Moab will not escape the judgment either. Great! But then Amos turned his guns on their sister kingdom to the south. Because Judah had spurned the word of the Lord and had not kept his commandments, Jerusalem would soon be overthrown. The people quieted down. Did Amos really mean it? But then, he came from there and he ought to know. At least he had not said anything about Israel itself. He wouldn't dare, would he?

> This is what the Lord says:
> Because of outrage after outrage committed by Israel
> I will not relent!
> For they have sold the innocent for a handful of silver,
> And needy men for a pair of shoes.
> They grind the faces of the poor into dust,
> And force the humble out of his rightful path.
> Father and son use the same temple-girl,
> And so defile my holy name.
> ....
> Is this not true, you children of Israel?
> This is the Lord himself speaking to you.
>
> You only have I chosen from all the nations of the earth.
> Therefore it is you whom I will punish for all your wrong-doings.[3]

You can be sure that Amos' popularity did not last beyond that. His message was immediately spurned and he was rejected as an upstart who didn't know the score. When he ran headlong into the top religious leader of the land, he was told to go back home and mind his own business.[4] Repentance is never popular preaching, especially to the Church.

Anyway, what do we have to confess? We are so ingrained in the habit of looking at the Church from *within* that we never see it from *without*. We are unable to see ourselves as we really are. This is true in every area of life. How different your business seems to you from inside it than it does to an outsider. You run it or work in it daily. You are behind the counter, but he is in front of it. Your home, now that you have lived in it a couple of years, also looks quite different than it did when you first set foot in it. We have been so long inside the Church that seeing ourselves and the Church from the outside will be a shock.

When it comes right down to looking at ourselves, we may have lifted the top of the box to take a peek, but then we closed the lid again quickly. We need a more thorough inventory than that. Not that I'm suggesting a morbid preoccupation with ourselves like a certain strain of Puritanism which majors on a horrified self-examination. That becomes somewhat like looking into an inner cesspool, and no one can keep that up indefinitely, just as it is impossible to sustain an emotion of fear or keep up a smile from ear to ear every second.

We are, of course, aware to some extent of our "inward and original corruption. . . . I was more loathsome in mine own eyes than was a toad. . . . Sin and corruption as naturally bubble out of my heart, as water would bubble out of a fountain."[5] When we become open to the word of God which tells us about man (and therefore about ourselves!) we cannot fail to admit to this darkness within.

Besides, has not Jesus evaluated man's heart as evil? "From within, out of the heart of men, proceed evil thoughts, adulteries, fornications, murders, thefts, covetousness, wickedness, deceit, lasciviousness, an evil eye, blasphemy, pride, foolishness. All these evil things come from within, and defile the man."[6] Will that not bring us to self-examination and confession? This realistic appraisal of man is most necessary in the Church.

Therefore we will not be overly surprised at the prejudice and bigotry we discover, nor the legalism, the overt anxieties, the rigidity, or even the hypocrisy which rears its ugly head. With our self-satisfactions and peacock pride we are not ready to change, but we must surely begin to make amends through confession.

Now this is precisely where we are in the habit of sweeping the dirt under the rug. We want so much to make the impression that our Christian house is clean. Does not Christianity change our lives? Is not Christ our Savior? We quote the Scripture that "if any man is in Christ he is a new creation," so must we not appear all new?[7] Then, how does it happen that we are not what we profess? Why is all this dust invading our Christian homes? Why are we continually tracking in more dirt? Why do the windows always look as if they need washing? If we vacuumed the place just a week ago, why does it seem like nothing has been cleaned this week? And why is the kitchen floor filled with scuff marks again? And again? And again?

But we must never admit any of this—just sweep it all under the rug. No one must suspect that our homes get just as dirty as those of our worldly neighbors. After all, everything is supposed to be *new!*

That is our dilemma. Let us admit that we Christians live by confession. Our lives get as messed up as anybody's. Why else do our prayers read that "we have left undone those things which we ought to have done; and we have done those things which we ought not to have done. And there is no health in us. But Thou, O Lord, have mercy upon us, miserable offenders"? Miserable offenders? Yes, and much more!

Why do our hymns repeat lines like: "Prone to wander, Lord, I feel it; prone to leave the God I love"? Or why does Lancelot Andrewes, that devout bishop of the seventeenth century, offer such confession in his *Private Devotions* as this: "The just falleth seven times a day, and I, an exceeding great sinner, seventy times seven. Lord, I repent, help Thou mine impenitence; and more, and still more, pierce Thou, rend, crush my heart. And remit, pardon, forgive all things that are grief unto me and offence of heart. Cleanse Thou me from secret faults, keep back Thy servant also from presumptuous sins. Magnify Thy mercies towards the utter sinner; and in season, Lord, say to me, Be of good cheer; thy sins are forgiven thee"?

Andrewes was no unimportant Christian. He was one of the men who prepared the translation of the King James version of the Bible. He was also the chaplain to Queen Elizabeth the First.

"If we walk in the light, as he is in the light, we have fellowship one with another, and the blood of Jesus Christ his Son cleanses us from all sin."[8] This is the realization that as we walk in the presence of God, we walk humbly, confessing our sins. The blood of Christ cleanses *as we walk in the light*. It is a present experience for Christians, a daily, even momentary acceptance of forgiveness.

Or else why should we be told to "pray without ceasing?"[9] Why this need to pray, which means keeping in touch with God, unless there is a purpose? Why practice the presence of God if all is well on the horizon of our Christian lives? Why should I bother to repent unless I am aware of my rebellious nature and the spirit of obstinacy which is still within me?

But the promise of this life of humility is that as we "draw near to God, He will draw near to us." How do we enter his presence? "Cleanse your hands, you sinners; and purify your hearts, you double minded. Be afflicted, and mourn, and weep. . . . Humble yourselves in the sight of the Lord."[10] Have we Christians listened to what is being said to us? Or do we so possess all the answers through our superb insight into the Bible that we have no need for confession?

The Church needs to take a cold douche of facts. No one in the world is interested in a proud Church. Neither does anyone enjoy Christians who claim to have all the answers. Only as we admit that we, too, are beggars in need of the grace of God will we be able to point others to the place where we have found bread. Our house is just as dirty and as empty as theirs. We have no corner on sanctity. The plain truth is that we are on the way, and on the way as beggars.

Martin Luther's last words were "We are beggars, that is true." You would expect him to list his accomplishments at the end of his life. Perhaps you would expect to hear him say: "Lord God Almighty, look upon thy servant now in mercy and truth. I have worked for thee all the days of my life. I have done thy will. I have resisted the evil of the existing church and exposed its doctrinal heresies. I have guided thy people into truth. Now, therefore, O Lord, because of my theological labors and the proclamation of thy word, receive me into everlasting rest, according to thy great promises in Jesus Christ, our Lord. Amen."

He did not say anything like that. Only "we are beggars, that is true." Being beggars means that we are always recipients of God's grace. Where there is no sin, there is no need of grace. But until our dying breath we can do no better than admit our beggarly condition. We are always like thieves who can only say at the end: "Remember me when thou comest into thy kingdom."[11] Beggars, all.

Traditionally we have said that the essence of sin is disobedience to God. Adam and Eve refused to believe the word of God and disobeyed him when they reached for the forbidden fruit. We have also thought of sin as transgression, the breaking of God's commandments. We have emphasized sin as revolt, the rebellion of the whole man against God, reaching out a fist toward heaven. Sin in Scripture is also falling short of the goal, missing the mark, not achieving perfection.

Even more severe, sin is sacrilege. "We poison the wine as He decants it into us; murder a melody He would play with us as the instrument. We caricature the self-portrait He would paint. Hence all sin, whatever else it is, is sacrilege," says C. S. Lewis.[12]

In another letter to Malcolm, Mr. Lewis points out that resentment is the reverse side of humility. Instead of humbling ourselves to ask for forgiveness, we fondle our resentments, returning to them again and again as a "relief from, or alternative to, humiliation."[13] So we are always taking that which God would give us and turning it to selfish ends. We poison the good. Beggars we are, and beggars *we remain.*

But there is a positive aspect here, too. As beggars we are free to receive. We acknowledge our indebtedness to him and thus we can receive with open hands his gifts of love and mercy. What if we were not beggars but businessmen? Our hands would remain closed! Through our own accomplishments we businessmen need not go begging. We have manufactured our own ethics and good deeds. The factory of our moral life has turned out good works, so we need not beg for anything. Why should we have to beg—even from God?

Beggars have nothing to boast of, no accomplishments. They make no pretenses. We beggars just live off the good will of Someone Else who promises to take care of us. We who name the name of Christ should be far more aware of our poverty than we are. Have we forgotten how we happened to become

Christians? Or do we think that being a Christian is something we have achieved, something of which we can boast that we are *in* and everybody else is *out?* Do we have a corner on the grace of God? Are we the manufacturers of his message to the world? Do we produce the love of God, wrap it up and dispatch it for a price? Hardly.

We are beggars all. If we will let that truth penetrate evangelical Christianity, it can only begin to drive us to God in humble confession. The person who fails to see his beggarly condition has never really met Jesus Christ, for he certainly needs no Savior in the present tense. Contrition and sorrow for sin have lost their meaning for him as present reality. Such an evangelical Christian is a false Christian, a weed among the wheat. He has, in fact, placed himself outside of the grace of God.

NOTES:

1. Soren Kierkegaard, *Purity of Heart Is To Will One Thing* (New York: Harper & Row., Inc., 1956), pp. 196,197.
2. Mark 1:14, 15.
3. Amos 2:6–8,11; 3:2. From J. B. Phillips, *Four Prophets* (New York: The Macmillan Company, 1963), pp. 7,8,9. See also Amos 1 and 2.
4. See Amos 7:10–13.
5. John Bunyan, *Grace Abounding to the Chief of Sinners.*
6. Mark 7:21–23.
7. II Cor. 5:17.
8. I John 1:7.
9. I Thess. 5:17.
10. Jas. 4:8–10.
11. Luke 13:42.
12. C. S. Lewis, *Letters to Malcolm* (New York: Harcourt, Brace & World, Inc., 1964), p. 96.
13. *Ibid.*, p. 95

20. The Spirit of Awareness

A NAZI soldier entered the place where Picasso's massive war mural was on display. The mural showed twisted shapes of grotesque figures by which Picasso was portraying man's inhumanity, man degenerating into heartless slaughter of his fellow man. The Nazi turned to a man standing there, not knowing him to be Picasso, and asked, "Who is responsible for these things?" To which Picasso replied: "You are."

The Christian must move beyond confession of known sins and failures to the awareness that he is really to blame for the poor showing of the Church. To an awareness that the failure of Christianity is not the fault of God, but results from each one of us being no better than we are. As the Apostle Paul said to the religiously conservative community of his time: "The name of God is blasphemed among the Gentiles through you."[1] Why is that truth seldom, if ever, heard among us?

A recent book by sociologists Charles Y. Glock and Rodney Stark is entitled *Christian Beliefs and Anti-Semitism.*[2] The authors, who are Lutherans, questioned almost three thousand people in the San Francisco area. They found a high degree of anti-Semitism in the churches, although "no church is deliberately fostering such prejudice." Whether this is true or not is hardly the question. It may be possible to disprove the authors' methods and findings. The fact remains, as has already been pointed out earlier, that prejudice, criticism and bigotry are the glue which hold some Christian(?) groups together. To be blind to all this is a denial of our continuing failure.

Consider another concrete example. A certain conservative church found itself in a changing neighborhood. This was a church which at its peak could boast over two thousand members and a vital ministry. From this fine congregation numerous sons and daughters went into the ministry and mission fields, and many are even now serving Christ ably. They first found Christ in that church. No doubt as they reflect on the sorry status of the present congregation they must shed bitter tears.

There are about six hundred members now, some of whom are Negroes. The worship service, however, only brings out about one hundred Caucasians and perhaps thirty Negroes. The white congregation's average age is sixty-five. There are no young families living in that area and only two couples drive back in who are around forty. The minister of youth is a student in seminary (white), the organist is a college student (white), and the choir director is young and white. There are no other white young people around. The Sunday school is ninety-nine percent Negro. Financial support is so low that only legacies left by a few have carried that church while it was operating in the red.

But why all this? Have the people not sensed the drift of the times? Have they been unaware of the changes in that neighborhood? And why are there no Negroes in the choir? Why do only a couple of Negroes teach in the Sunday school, and that only because no other whites could be found? Why are there no Negro ushers, but only white-haired or balding men? Why are there no Negroes on any of the official boards?

It is hardly possible to point to the incompetence, inexperience or unreliability of the Negro—if there be such. We should rather point the finger at the rigidity, fear, hostility and prejudice operating in the heart of the white congregation. When Negroes were told some years ago, "Wouldn't you rather worship with your own?" is it any wonder now that the community is not ready to jump on that evangelical bandwagon? (*Is* that church evangelical?) And is it any wonder that the neighborhood remains hostile toward this bulwark of fundamentalism? For when their gymnasium was beginning to attract more Negroes than Caucasians that great church tore the thing down, rather than have it misused!

Such evils exist in churches everywhere, but that particular church is doomed. It has resisted the power of the Spirit. It has refused to listen to the word of God. It has failed to preach the good news to every person; while the people came to worship on Sundays, blasphemy, disobedience, rebellion—yes, and sacrilege arose from that sanctuary.

Is that judgment too severe? Every Christian ought to weep over that church. That church's failure belongs not to that one church; it is *our* failure. We all contribute to the debris of sin, and for anyone to say, "I wouldn't have done that" is to miss the point. We *have* done that, or something like that, if not something far worse. The causes of evil are deep within the human heart. Prejudice and all our human ills originate there. Until a Christian allows the Lord of all to change him, no transformation will take place. Confession is the first step, and awareness of our condition, the second.

Blind men will lead others into the ditch. Those who have their eyes open, or rather, have had their eyes opened by Someone Else, have become aware. This process of opening our eyes, how does it come about? How can we who are blind receive our vision, apart from the miracle of new birth? How, unless we're truly converted? "Except a man be born again, he cannot *see* the kingdom of God."[3] But does not conversion itself mean an about face, a complete capitulation of one's former position to a new, opposite and positive faith? Vision follows birth.

So birth, as the word implies, is only the beginning. There must be growth, and as we grow in our new life our eyes will certainly be opened. Have you ever noticed how children observe and receive and are constantly exploring? They have their eyes wide open to an ever new world, not wanting to miss anything. Adults, too, have to be continually alert. While driving, a moment's relaxation may cause an accident; while watching a ball game, by a turn of the head you may miss the home run. We need to keep this sharp edge on life. But how? How can we be continually aware? How can we be alert spiritually?

The traditional answers to these questions are usually that we must pray, read the Bible, attend church, witness, and put our faith into action. These traditional answers need not be changed, although in the Sermon on the Mount Jesus throws new light on them. He discusses such religious matters as prayer, fasting, and giving and demonstrates how empty they are by themselves. If Christianity is practiced to impress either man or God, if observances are kept out of a sense of obligation, or if religious acts are performed for recognition and reward, then the whole business is really for nothing. It would have been better not to be so religious since these acts have only made us hypocritical. And religious hypocrites are unaware, insincere and insensitive.

But how can a person change himself? How can the person who has been shot down by some (if not all) of the points raised in this book change his thinking and life? This is the human dilemma with which education, philosophy, psychology, sociology, and the humanities have all wrestled, trying to gain insight and understanding—and even to find God.

The Christian Church has always said the answer comes through faith in Christ. But we are particularly concerned now with those who have such faith in Christ; they have been "born again" and say they are Christians. We must ask whether this faith in Christ is a living reality? What does it mean to receive the gift of the Holy Spirit, God's Spirit? Can a Christian congregation believe in God on the one hand and reject their neighbors on the other, like that church in the changing neighborhood?

How can we have faith in Christ unless we draw near to Christ? How can we continue in his favor unless we become sensitive to his divine will? How is it possible to receive the Spirit of God unless we willingly examine ourselves and become aware of our gaping needs? Awareness is the true meaning of living by faith. It is openness to God's revelation and listening for his direction. This awareness is not an extra, like an additional vitamin you may take or not take, depending on your diet. Rather, this is the ground on which we stand, the God in whom we live and move and have our being, who wants to communicate himself to us—the God with whom we have to do.

"Religion isn't something to be added to our other duties, and thus make our lives yet more complex. The life with God is the center of life, and all else is remodelled and integrated by it."[4]

Have you ever taken a walk in the country without ever seeing anything? You didn't have to be blind, but you just didn't see the mountains, the sky, the clouds. The birds didn't interest you, much less the insects, the tiny flowers in the grass beside the road, or the dirt under your feet. You were aware in some remote way that you were walking in the country. (You were not in the city. You were not driving but walking. You were not with people but alone. You were not in the noise of traffic but in the quiet of the open air.) You were aware of all these facts and yet you were never really awake to your surroundings.

You do not have to be a biologist to be conscious and aware of your walk in the country, analyzing every weed with "this is that." Such an attitude becomes mechanically analytical and actually gets in the way of awareness. It is analysis instead of experience. The scientist classifies, the mathematician calculates, the weather expert predicts, the newscaster reports.

What is this awareness during a simple walk? It cannot be put down in words. The moment you put down words you spoil something. The moment you say: "This and this is how I feel," you erase that feeling. Through analyzing and thinking about it, reality stops. And yet it is possible in an ordinary walk to become open to nature, and through nature to the presence of God. At the same time you become aware of the murkiness which resides within.

Such is the experience of the psalmist who considers God's handiwork during night and day, who meditates on the holiness of God and is led to his own sense of failure. "The heavens declare the glory of God; and the firmament sheweth his handiwork. . . . The law of the Lord is perfect, converting the soul. . . . The fear of the Lord is clean, enduring forever. . . . Cleanse thou me from secret faults. Keep back thy servant also from presumptuous sins."[5]

"Who has ears to hear, let him hear," said Jesus.[6] What does this mean? We all have ears to receive impressions and sounds. But how much penetrates to be recorded within, entering the real self? What are we really able to hear? Chinese music is just a lot of noise to those who are not Chinese. The reason for this is that the Chinese have thirty-two times a finer pitch in their music than Westerners are accustomed to. Consequently we cannot really "hear" their variations. We have ears, but what we hear sounds jumbled.

Is it surprising that Jesus repeated this one saying often? "Who has ears to hear, let him hear." Are we able to hear the truth about ourselves? Are we willing to let the Bible speak to us? Are we ready to listen to good friends who are courageous enough to talk plainly; or even to enemies who do not seem to mind telling us what they think? Are we willing to admit not only what is wrong, but also move in the direction of that which is right? How else can we deal with all that is phony in our lives?

Most of us have a cutoff point when it comes to listening. We hear only that which we want to hear. We stop listening even to God, when the going gets tough. But this means that we will never make any advances in the Christian life! It also means we do not really intend to be serious Christians. Of course we have followed God's will at times, but why not at all times? Of course we have asked for his guidance in certain situations, but why have we not counted this Holy One within us the most precious thing in the world?

There is a story about a man who was asked, "Can you lend me five dollars?"

"What did you say?" He replied.

"Can you lend me five dollars?"

"Come around to the other ear, and ask me what you are trying to ask me. I'm a little hard of hearing."

The man came around and said: "Can you lend me ten dollars?"

"Come back to five dollars, will you?"

We hear what we want to hear. But we also hear that which we pretend not to. When do you stop listening to God? What is the point at which you turn down the volume and look only at the picture, and then proceed to turn the picture off also? Awareness certainly involves a willingness to heed God. Even when we are no longer willing.

The reason we are not going anywhere in our Christianity is not because God is dumb but because we have closed our ears. It is not that God has nothing to say to us, but simply that we have lost the desire to listen any longer. According to Jesus we have the capacity for hearing. That is encouraging. Change is not impossible as long as we have the capacity and are willing to be open, even though instinctively and quite naturally we'd rather close up shop.

Jesus said to the religious people of his time: "My word has no place in you."[7] It is entirely possible to receive some of God's word (as they did) and yet refuse the revelation we really need. It is possible to worship and pray and believe and yet not receive the truth Christ wants us to hear. Are we aware that this possibility is real enough? "Why do you not understand my speech? Even because you cannot hear my word."[8] But we can hear it if we will turn the volume up.

"We Western peoples are apt to think our great problems are external, environmental. We are not skilled in the inner life, where the real roots of our problem lie. . . . The outer distractions of our interests reflect an inner lack of integration of our own lives. . . . We have hints that there is a way of life vastly richer and deeper than all this hurried existence, a life of unhurried serenity and peace and power. If only we could slip over into that Center! If only we could find the Silence which is the source of sound! . . . Life is meant to be lived from a Center, a divine Center. Each one of us can live such a life of amazing power and peace and serenity, of integration and confidence and simplified multiplicity, on one condition—that is, *if we really want to.*"[9]

That old advice from the psalms to "wait upon the Lord"

does not mean patient resignation. We do not have to sit until God comes to us, wondering if he will. Rather if we say to someone: "I'll meet you at that place at nine, and if I happen to be a few minutes late, please wait until I get there," we mean, "you can expect me." The important thing is not the mere waiting but the expectation that a meeting will take place. "My soul wait thou only upon God; for my expectation is from him."[10] Such ears are tuned to the Eternal to hear sounds which we have not dared to listen to before.

In the long run (and this is the only *long* run) we will be judged for our awareness. "And what is the point of calling me 'Lord, Lord,' without doing what I tell you to do? Let me show you what the man who comes to me, hears what I have to say, and puts it into practice, is really like. He is like a man building a house, who dug down to rock bottom and laid the foundation of his house upon it. Then when the flood came and the flood water swept down upon that house, it could not shift it because it was properly built."[11]

He who has ears to hear let him become aware.

NOTES:

1. Rom. 2:24.
2. Published by Harper & Row, Inc., New York, 1966.
3. John 3:3.
4. Thomas R. Kelly, *A Testament of Devotion* (New York: Harper & Row, Inc., 1941), p. 121.
5. Psa. 19:1,7,9,12,13.
6. Matt. 13:9.
7. John 8:37.
8. John 8:43.
9. Thomas R. Kelly, *ibid.,* p. 114–116.
10. Psa. 62:5.
11. Luke 6:46–48 (Phillips).

21.
The Way of Honesty

DARE we be honest? Is it possible to come clean as Christians?

Whenever I have asked another Christian the question, "What's wrong with the Church?" there has been an immediate, almost electric response. His face lights up and the problem is that he hardly knows where to begin. There seems to be so much wrong with the Church that the question is overwhelming.

We can freely talk with one another about these ills, and we are often willing to discuss such matters in small groups. Dare we be open before the public? Are we allowed to talk about our failures as human beings, or is this not acceptable? Should we keep up a smiling front as pleasant but sacrilegious hypocrites?

That we are not perfect, we know. Why suppress it then? Why suppress the fact that the boys in the victorious overcoming group are often the most hellish bunch of all? Why suppress the fact that Christians blow up at mealtimes in their homes, shouting at each other and hardly behaving as Christians? Or that Christian parents do not want their teenage sons or daughters discussing personal problems with their minister because it would tend to incriminate those parents? Why suppress the fact that many a young fellow may be truly converted and yet six months after his conversion still continue to masturbate? Why suppress the truth that many Christians struggle with their old habits and at times slip back into former ways, including alcoholism, gambling, or some sexual deviation? Why suppress the fact that a Bible-carrying Christian sits in a church holding hands with his girl friend, while his wife and child are at home since they do not belong to that church, and that an affair far beyond holding hands has been sanctioned for them by their interpretation of the Bible?

Cannot such stories be repeated ad infinitum, so that we finally begin to shake our heads and wonder where the real Christians are? Are they only old ladies or young children? I don't believe that for a moment. I must say again that I have met many devout and sincere Christians. But the bad things about us cannot remain suppressed. Besides, they get out into the community, and scandals make the papers. Certainly our failures are gossiped about, and because of this many an ethical person turns up his nose at the Church and will not have anything to do with Christianity. They are looking for honesty in Christians, these people in the world. And, strangely enough, we Christians expect it also from one another as well as from ourselves.

We must be able to level with each other. If we cannot bring ourselves to do this among ourselves, how can we ever face the world? If we cannot find acceptance among our own Christian fellowship, where else will we ever find it? So, this suppression has to come to an end among ourselves before we are ready to confess to the world what is the truth about us Christians. But as soon as we are able to be honest, the world will take notice of us.

A minister was ready to give up the ministry. In desperation he made one final attempt, forcing himself to go to a neighboring pastor. After a good talk, he made this comment: "You are the first minister from whom I have felt acceptance." He did not quit the ministry. Why had he experienced such rejection from fellow ministers? Was it his own fault that he felt like a loner? Or was it so hard to belong to the fellowship of those who with him were children of God? As long as we fail so miserably to accept one another we are not yet honest.

"He who is alone with his sin is utterly alone. It may be that Christians, notwithstanding corporate worship, common prayer, and all their fellowship in service, may still be left to their loneliness. . . . Though they have fellowship with one another as believers and as devout people, they do not have fellowship as the undevout, as sinners. The pious fellowship permits no one to be a sinner. So everybody must conceal his sin from himself and from the fellowship. We dare not be sinners. Many Christians are unthinkably horrified when a real sinner is suddenly discovered among the righteous. So we remain alone with our sin, living in lies and hypocrisy. The fact is that we *are* sinners!"[1]

The basic requirement for Alcoholics Anonymous is self-honesty. A person must only be willing to admit that he is an alcoholic and unable to handle alcohol. Other groups have followed in their tracks—gamblers anonymous, divorcées anonymous, even overeaters anonymous, and others. The principle is always the same. A man gets up at A.A. and introduces his story with this identifying tag: "My name is Joe [or Harry, or Jim]. I'm an alcoholic." That opening statement is a revelation and a humiliation.

What is the Church but a fellowship of sinners anonymous? Our only qualification for belonging is the admission of our revolt against God, our shocking disobedience of his will, and our turning of everything good into self-satisfaction. We are not the fine, upstanding citizens of the community. We are not the good society. We are not in ourselves qualified to belong (to God?) at all. Not our vocations, not our stations in life, not our places in the community and certainly not any economic bracket or membership of a certain race qualifies us. Only one fact—we are sinners in need of a Savior. "My name is ______. I'm a sinner. That's why I am here." I may be "saved," but I'm still a sinner. That is the honest truth.

Since we've brought Alcoholics Anonymous into this, let's take a brief look at the twelve steps which are the heart of the

A.A. program. These steps continually turn to the question of honesty, as if they are observing it from all its angles—a fact that may amaze many Christians.

(1) "We admitted we were powerless over alcohol—that our lives had become unmanageable." Is this not confession which brings a person to a new road? But the honest member of A.A. continues with this confession all his journey long.

(2) "We came to believe that a Power greater than ourselves could restore us to sanity." This is honesty toward God, and the admission that we cannot attain sanity alone.

(3) "We made a decision to turn our wills and our lives over to the care of God, as we understood him." As Christians we understand God to be revealed in Christ, but here again the crisis of self-surrender becomes the turning point.

(4) "We made a searching and fearless moral inventory of ourselves." The place to begin spiritually is not with our virtues but with our vices. That is the only honest basis on which we can proceed in the Christian life.

(5) "We admitted to God, to ourselves, and to one other human being, the exact nature of our wrongs." No deceptions, only the admission of our wrongs. In all of this we are willing to face up to the plague of the heart. We dare to be sinners.

(6) "We were entirely ready to have God remove all these defects of character." Generally we justify our wrongs and make excuses. We build fences of protection around ourselves. Here is the decision to turn ourselves over to God's direction.

(7) "We humbly asked him to remove our shortcomings." How many lifelong Christians have avoided this simple challenge to allow pride, fear, lust and resentment to be dealt with positively?

(8) "We made a list of all persons we had harmed, and became willing to make amends to them all." There is honesty in human relationships.

(9) "We made direct amends to such people wherever possible, except when to do so would injure them or others." Jesus said that unless we are right with our fellow man, we cannot worship God in sincerity and truth.[2] Our first task is to make things right.

(10) "We continued to take personal inventory and when we were wrong promptly admitted it." Underline *continued,* and *promptly.*

(11) "We sought through prayer and meditation to improve our conscious contact with God, as we understood him, praying only for knowledge of his will for us and the power to carry that out." When lines are open, communication is established. Only the person who walks in the light will confront his own darkness.

(12) "Having had a spiritual experience as the result of these steps, we tried to carry this message to alcoholics, and to practice these principles in all our affairs." The sharing of the good news is the ultimate result of honest confrontation. It is also a factor in continuing with this humiliating self-appraisal.

If there is one word from the New Testament which underlines all this, it would be: "Examine yourselves whether you are in the faith."[3] This is addressed to Christians, who are called saints,[4] that is, people who are set apart through baptism and the gift of the Spirit to live for Christ. At the same time Christians are sinners, and as such they realize their imperfections and failures. Only this self-honesty brings us into the flow of God's grace through Jesus Christ. Our situation could be summarized as one in which the new (which is already there as present reality) and the old (which still remains until death) are in constant conflict. "Strange," confesses Luther, "though I am saved from sin, I am not saved from sinning."

Paul (who told Christians to examine themselves) said of himself that he had not yet attained. He had not reached perfection. After twenty years' experience as a missionary he made this astonishing statement: "I bruise my own body and make it know its master, for fear that after preaching to others I should find myself rejected."[5] Although the Christian conflict is destined for victory, which Paul himself taught (just as members of A.A. are not called to suffer further defeats), to suppose that the Christian life can be anything other than conflict is sheer illusion.

Let's be honest, then, about the conflicts, for only through honesty will the Church become a society of acceptance. Until we can experience this spirit of acceptance, the Church will suffer from suppressed fears. We are dying spiritually from our lack of sincere fellowship because we close the lace curtains of a victorious life to cover our inner weaknesses and to keep out the light, and the fresh air, of God's Spirit. Our strength lies only in the willingness to be open with one another and with God. Some Christians in Africa have this motto: "We walk with the roof off before God and the walls down before our brothers."

Some find a renewal of life in Christian group therapy, but they are mighty few. Those who do, however, have dared to be honest in a small group, and therefore they can also be honest before the world, too. They make no pretense. They wear no mask, even the mask of a good Christian. They practice the truth that God has accepted us *as sinners* (just as A.A. has accepted every member as alcoholics), and they need make no bones about it.

When Job prayed to God after the loss of all his possessions and the sudden tragic death of all his children and grandchildren, he was still able to bless the name of the Lord. "In all this did not Job sin with his lips."[6] But after his friends came to see him, Job let out all his hostility: "Let the day perish wherein I was born. . . . Why died I not from the womb?"[7] And more. Still he did not sin with his lips because he was not afraid to be honest before God. He did not attempt to hide any of his feelings (could he hide them from God anyway?) and he expressed his pent-up anger. This honest dealing with himself brought him to a far greater revelation of God than he had to begin with.

The closer a person gets to God, the more honest he will be about himself, and therefore the more grace he experiences. Grace is only grace when it is not deserved, when it is not worked for. And this is precisely the point! Our honesty before God which brings us to Jesus Christ is the only "lever" that will release the flow of God's love. The expression of our need opens our lives to his power. So the sick go to the doctor and outcasts come to Christ to enter the kingdom. So the humble are heard in heaven, and life's failures become the salt of the earth.

John Robertson of Glasgow had been a preacher for forty years. But he lost his glow, felt himself a failure, and decided to resign. "O God," he prayed after a long time of indecision, "forty years ago thou didst commission me, but I have blundered and failed and I want to resign this morning." He broke down into tears, and as he humbled himself it seemed as if God gave him this answer: "John Robertson, it's true I commissioned you forty years ago and it's true you have blundered and failed, but you are not to resign your commission, but to re-sign your commission." Such material God always uses as his instruments.

Is it strange? You would expect the salt of the earth to be the accomplished, sophisticated leaders of men, the finest, the cultured, the highest ethically. To the contrary, the salt of the earth are the humble, the suffering, the empty, the spiritually poverty-stricken—in other words, sinners anonymous. This is the truth of Christianity which need not be camouflaged under superficial performances. The meek inherit the earth.

When we forget these basic truths given to us by Jesus Christ, we only continue to steer ourselves into our present dilemma. The only way out is honesty with ourselves and one another and God. Perhaps we have to begin with God, for as we become honest with him without faking, we learn from him to be honest with ourselves. Nothing prevents God from loving us. He will not turn his back on us in spite of our waywardness. He has demonstrated his unchangeable love once and for all in the life and death of his only Son. We cannot help but marvel all our lives long that such grace is freely given. This is the greatness of the good news, where all sham ends. The misery of a sinner and the mercy of God!

Now as we learn to face ourselves, we see the things that need changing. We are ready to hear the word of God for ourselves, and so we can become truthful with one another, accepting and being accepted. The fellowship which has learned to be genuine will not be shunned by the man of the world. He will take note of sinners anonymous.

> Confession in the presence of a brother is the profoundest kind of humiliation. It hurts, it cuts a man down, it is a dreadful blow to pride. To stand there before a brother as a sinner is an ignominy that is almost unbearable. In the confession of concrete sins the old man dies a painful, shameful death before the eyes of a brother. . . .
>
> Jesus Christ himself . . . suffered the scandalous, public death of a sinner in our stead. He was not ashamed to be crucified for us as an evildoer. It is nothing else but our fellowship with Jesus Christ that leads us to the ignominious dying that comes in confession, in order that we may in truth share in his Cross. The Cross of Jesus Christ destroys all pride.[8]

The wife of a minister became disillusioned with the Church. "I was perhaps only six or seven, but I've never forgotten the moment I first felt the presence of God—in a church. Unfortunately, the life of a minister's wife has practically destroyed that for me. . . . The organizational church is a fascinating game, but the spirit of the true Church is not there! . . . One by one my idols fell, my refuges dissolved in the cold light of logic. . . . I gradually came to understand that I must find God again—or perhaps for the first time for myself. . . . I have built a wall of pain and fear and disillusionment."

And so during a Good Friday service she did: "I looked at the people, struggling, human and sinful, even as I, yet reaching toward God; and I heard the first compelling phrase—'Come! Let us kneel, in sorrow and contrition. . . . My sins, my sins, my Savior, they take such hold on me.' (Dear God! Who knew this better than I!) I know they are forgiven, but their pain to me is all the grief and anguish they laid, my Lord, on thee. . . . I was only aware of sorrow, and forgiveness, and soul-shaking humility, as I saw the people come to Communion—the urban, sophisticated people, with tears streaming down their faces, and hope in their eyes."[9]

"It is God's nature to make something out of nothing. That is why God cannot make anything out of him who is not yet nothing."[10]

NOTES:

1. Dietrich Bonhoeffer, *Life Together* (New York: Harper & Row, Inc., 1954), p. 110.
2. See Matt. 5:23,24.
3. II Cor. 13:5.
4. II Cor. 1:2.
5. I Cor. 9:27 (*New English Bible*).
6. Job 2:10.
7. Job 3:3,11.
8. Dietrich Bonhoeffer, *op. cit.*, p. 114.
9. William Douglas, *Ministers' Wives* (New York: Harper & Row, Inc., 1965), pp. 65,66.
10. Martin Luther.

22. The Centrality of the Bible

ONE of the strengths of the Church has been its emphasis on the Bible. The Bible has always been central in the pulpit as the minister stands behind it and interprets it through his sermon. The congregation expects preaching that is biblically oriented. This fact in itself should turn out to be the salvation of Protestants.

There is however a continuing battle among Sunday school publishers over educational materials. The evangelicals assert that major denominations have moved away from Scripture and are not thoroughly Biblical. The new education boys argue that they are just as Bible oriented but they simply do not use quotations and proof texts. They major on the implications of Scripture, to which the evangelicals counter that unless you have the Bible you *don't* have the Bible in your curriculum.

In spite of all the educational material, however, and all their Sunday school education, Protestants still have an abysmal ignorance of the Bible. All most people know about their Bibles can be reduced to the Ten Commandments and that Jesus died for our sins. Little else. In my own experience with congregations I have always felt I could not refer to either the story of the good Samaritan or the prodigal son without explaining who they were, what they did, who told the story and why. A quotation from Hosea would get the same blank response as a reference to the code of Hammurabi. And most Protestants wouldn't know that second Hezekiah is not a book in the Bible.

Though these examples may sound extreme such ignorance is actually widespread. There were always people in my classes preparing for membership who had never heard some of the most familiar stories Jesus told, and who had no idea what the New Testament actually has to say. There is a gaping need in the Church which stands for the Bible—the need to teach the Bible meaningfully, to encourage its reading devotionally—and to study it. Ask any church group on any day how many have ever read the Bible through, and in most churches the response will be quite meager.

The idea still persists (and perhaps it is a holdover from medieval times) that the clergy alone can interpret or understand the Bible properly. So, it's better not to tamper with the Bible too much. You might get confused. The Reformation was a revolt against all such nonsense. It was an attempt to put the Bible into the hands of the common people. Now it *is* in our hands, but we don't pick it up! The laymen's movement of our time, which hopes to overcome all this, has not yet succeeded in bringing the Reformation hope into reality.

Then there is a minority group who do know their Bible. They are the faithful students who are making an attempt to be open to God's revelation. Sometimes their knowledge changes their lives, but not always. They often approach Scripture with their own ideas as to what it has to say, and therefore in their blindness do not receive the word of God at all. Their doctrinal fancies block off the possibility of insight. They look on Scripture as a book which dispenses righteousness mechanically, much as a coffee machine pours a cup of coffee after your dime has gone into the slot.

These people not only have a rigid attitude but they are often afraid. They fear the liberals, the critics. They fear that those who want to lighten the ship of Christianity to keep it afloat may actually succeed in sinking it. However, this fear is misplaced and unnecessary. C. S. Lewis makes an apt comment at this point.

> Liberal Christianity can only supply an ineffectual echo to the massive chorus of agreed and admitted unbelief. Don't be deceived by the fact that this echo so often "hits the headlines." That is because attacks on Christian doctrine . . . become news when the attacker is a clergyman; just as a very commonplace protest against make-up would be news if it came from a film star.
>
> By the way, did you ever meet, or hear of, anyone who was converted from skepticism to a "liberal" or 'demythologised' Christianity? I think that when unbelievers come in at all, they come in a good deal further.[1]

It may seem to be an act of faith, this holding on to the Bible in face of the critics, but it may also be a lack of faith. Indeed we may refuse to listen to the gains of scholarship because we are lazy, or just afraid of any exposé which may finish off Christianity! Is God dead or alive? Is Jesus, the Christ, the Son of God, or not? Or is this whole thing the biggest hoax ever perpetrated on the human race? If the critics are right, if the new theologians prove that evangelicals are through, if the Bible is an old book with outdated views—what then? If we live in constant fear of such things we may slip into the error of regarding the word of God as a fetish. We may idolize it, closing our eyes to it in nervous anxiety.

In a brilliant analogy Helmut Thielicke has put it this way:

> Not a few of my fundamentalist brethren, whom I seek in honest love and certainly not in pharisaic pride, remind me of the disciples on the ship crossing the Sea of Galilee with the Lord on board. There they are by themselves—for, of course, the Lord is sleeping—prowling about the ship, listening to the creaking in the ship's sides and peering from the railings into the water to see whether they can discover some Bult-* or frogman down there boring a hole in the ship's side. When the Lord

* The reference is to the modern theologian Rudolf Bultmann.

finally woke up, to his amazement he saw his men aimlessly and excitedly running about instead of being at their nautical stations, performing their regular duties, while the ship had obviously gotten off course.

Then he asked them, "Why aren't you paying attention to the course instead of running about as you are?"

They answered, "We're looking out to see whether some Bult- or frogman is boring into our ship."

And the Lord said: "Why should that interest you?"

The disciples replied, "But, dear Lord, how can you ask such a thing? If the ship gets a hole in it, the water will come in!"

And the Lord said, "Yes, and what then?'"

The disciples said, "Why, the ship will go down."

Whereupon the Lord said, "So that's what you are afraid of! O men of little faith, don't you know that the ship can never go down as long as I am sleeping in it?"[2]

The Scriptures are the ship in which our Lord sleeps, so to speak. Since *he* is in that ship we are interested in the ship itself. But which is more important, the Lord or the ship? And as long as he promises to be with us to the end, why should we live in fear?

The Bible has become for so many a book demanding our allegiance without leading us into a relationship with God himself. This means we are not doing justice to its message—an offer to enter as free children into a relationship with our heavenly Father. It is a pure neglect of that message. The Bible is a record of that which God has done for man, in which we learn where we came from, why we are here and where we are going. We begin to understand that we have gone astray from God into a far country, and that we have rebelled against him. But the good news is that God wants us to come back home. He has personally entered this world to exhibit his love in Jesus Christ. He has opened the door for our return. This is the theme of the Bible. To miss God's call into that new life is to miss entirely God's word to man.

Overcoming both our ignorance and our fear may put us on

the road to renewal. The Bible must become meaningful to us not simply as a religious book, nor as an extra, but as basic to everything. It has the power through the Spirit of God to work influentially to change any willing person.

For example. Suppose an insecure person has no feelings of belonging, no assurance of being accepted. He may have been reared in an average home situation with a certain measure of love. But he still feels terribly insecure. Now he becomes a Christian and reads the Bible. The Bible communicates a message of security. It tells him—him of all people—that God loves him and that Jesus died for everyone. He may be taught the doctrine of eternal security, which means that once he has become a child of God he can never be disowned by him; no matter what he does, he is eternally secure. This teaching can bring great comfort and security since, as Jesus taught, "no man is able to pluck you out of my Father's hand."[3]

And yet has the full message of the Bible penetrated this person's life? He may still have skimmed only the surface, particularly if he remains insecure. What then? He does not need more doctrine, but he must begin to apply the truth that he knows directly to his problem. He must see that the Bible is not merely a book of theology but that its truths must affect him where he is the weakest. The Bible speaks to our insecurity. It tells us we are loved and accepted—we belong to God. Jesus receives us as we are and therefore we really know that we belong to him, even with all our annoying failures.

When this really happens through the Bible, it means that God is speaking to us from his word. Then the Bible is no longer some extra security like an outboard motor for a sailboat, but the very sail itself. (The wind blowing the sail is of God—the Holy Spirit—while we still keep our hands on the ropes to steer our course.) The Bible then becomes relevant indeed.

"To be with the Bible? I dare not! If I read it—the first passage I come upon is the best—I am bound immediately. It asks me (yes, it is just as if God himself asked me) have you done what you read? And then, yes, then I am caught, then it is either to act at once or immediately make a humiliating admission."[4]

All this leads me to say a word about *how* to read that book through which God speaks to us. A certain man had been in Jerusalem for the holidays and was heading back to his own country. He was reading a portion of the Bible, but he was not very successful. Then he saw a hitchhiker, who not only requested a ride, but who had the impertinence to peer at his Bible and ask him: "Do you understand what you are reading?"

The man was taken aback: "How can I?" he said almost spontaneously. "Someone has to interpret this thing to me. The Bible is a difficult book, you know, and I'm having a hard time."

The hitchhiker then began to explain the Scriptures. The man listened eagerly. "Tell me," he asked, "who is the prophet talking about in this passage? About himself or about someone else?"

Then Philip began at the same Scripture and preached to him Jesus.[5]

Like a watermark in stationery, Jesus is the heart of all Scripture. By grasping this theme of the Bible we will know how to proceed in reading it.

First, plan to read the Bible through. Why not? You need to get an overall view. The Bible is not like a phone book to be thumbed through for a verse (or number). Begin with the life of Jesus. Read the Gospels first. Then proceed to the book of the Acts, which tells the story of the early Christians. Next try the letters of the New Testament and finish with the book of the Revelation. There isn't that much. You may not grasp everything too well, but you will surely gain even through this first reading.

Now you are ready to get acquainted with the history of the Jewish people in the books of Genesis through Esther. (But the New Testament should be first so that you do not get bogged down and quit in Leviticus.) It is one majestic and fascinating story unless you get stuck in the genealogies or become overly worried about all those specifications for sacrifices. Skip those areas if you wish and stick to the story.

In the meanwhile you should have begun reading some psalms and proverbs, rummaging around in the worship literature of the Old Testament. Finish up with the prophets. The main point is to have a plan. Use any good translation. I lean toward Phillips and *The New English Bible* for the New Testament but have not found anything that vastly improves on the King James version for the Old. (The Amplified version provides help for additional studies.)

Second, take notes on what you read. Mark, underline, or put notes in the margins of your Bible. Use it as a book ought to be used, and you will retain so much more of it. The hourglass reader allows his reading to run in and out. The sponge reader soaks it all up and returns it quickly, only a little dirtier. The jelly bag reader allows the pure to pass through and retains only the refuse. But an archaeologist digs only for that which has value, as a driller for oil searches for that precious substance. What are you looking for? Reading can change the person who enters into dialogue with God.

Third, read the Bible not for merit but to receive God's message for yourself. That may require several chapters, or it may take only a couple of verses. A businessman may type a favorite verse and keep it on his desk. A housewife may place an open Bible at a familiar spot and while she does her housework look at it from time to time. Sometimes, like Charles Spurgeon, you can live on a promise for weeks. More often, however, you need daily bread, for which the Lord's prayer teaches us to ask.

"Human knowledge must be understood to be loved, but divine knowledge must be loved to be understood."[6] Even Immanuel Kant is quoted as having said: "A single line in the Bible has consoled me more than all the books I ever read besides."

In explaining his writing of the screenplay for the filming of the first episode of the Bible, the distinguished author Christopher Fry wrote: "However well you know the Bible—and it was very much a part of family reading when I was a boy—

there is almost no end to discovering how much there is still to think about. In planning the film we read and brooded on the text over and over again, and haven't yet got to the end of what we can find there."[7]

For Christians to make the message of the Bible relevant to the world, they must first allow it to become relevant to themselves.

NOTES.

1. C. S. Lewis, *Letters to Malcolm* (New York: Harcourt, Brace & World, Inc., 1964), p. 119.
2. Helmut Thielicke, *Between Heaven and Earth* (New York: Harper & Row, Inc., 1965), pp. 33,34.
3. John 10:29.
4. Kierkegaard.
5. The story is taken from Acts 8:27–38.
6. Blaise Pascal.
7. Christopher Fry, from his preface to *The Bible* (New York: Pocket Books, Inc., 1966), p. 5.

23.
A New Look at Jesus

OVER the years our image of Jesus has grown healthier and happier. Early Christian art represented Jesus as the troubled and meditative Savior. In medieval times his face was stern and dark and he appeared as the Judge. The Renaissance painted a weeping Christ, spattered with blood, suffering. The nineteenth century gave us the Victorian Christ, beautified and pink cheeked.

But now he is depicted like a religious weakling, soft, somewhat emaciated, even effeminate. His complexion is pasty and his mouth prettily rouged. His curly golden hair falls girlishly over his shoulders, and his long flowing robes place him in the long ago and far away. He does not smile, he does not speak, he does not compel. He does nothing! The picture has turned into pure sentiment.

"The radicals within the Church from Kierkegaard to Bonhoeffer have rejected this comfortable version of Christ, as they have rejected the idea that the Christian religion can be a comfortable one, in the modern definition of that abused word. And this surely suggests the basic difference between the kind of religion the establishment practices and true Christianity, which came into being as a difficult, dangerous, radical, uncomfortable, shattering, but also vastly stimulating and exciting way of life."[1]

A painting hanging in my office has elicited all sorts of comment. It represents Christ as suffering in agony on the cross. His face is distorted, his breathing belabored. Many a person has remarked: "Why is there so much suffering in that picture? Is this how you see Christ?" That painting does not fit in with the current notion of the carefree Jesus.

We have also failed to see Jesus as the great disturber. Why have we grown so accustomed to his face? Why have we settled for an easy Christ, who allows himself to be worshiped but does not demand that we follow him, listen to him, or obey him? These words are carved over a church door in Germany:

You call me the Way and walk me not,
You call me the Life and live me not,
You call me Master and obey me not,
If I condemn you, blame me not!

You call me Bread and eat me not,
You call me Truth and believe me not,
You call me Lord and serve me not,
If I condemn you, blame me not!

We have talked about the presence of Christ as something soothing and peaceful, rather like a fog that will settle over us and blot out all sharp edges and distinctions. Our Western emphasis on peace of mind has combined with the mysticism of the East to influence our thinking, so that we imagine an experience of God will fabricate a blissful union. In reality, when God confronts us we may develop some bad blisters. The prophets experienced uprooting and agony from their response to God's call. The apostles were often shocked in the presence of Jesus.[2]

Jesus' presence is not always so welcome. We call upon him in prayer and his first reply to our request may be: "Why have you been evading me for so long?" But only out of such a rebuke can we be stabbed awake. If we are not disturbed, we will never go beyond our happy dreams. A safe Jesus turns out to be nothing but fantasy. We need a new look at Jesus.

On the other hand there are those Christians who consider Jesus only as stern and judgmatic. They see him only as one who must be obeyed, feared and respected. There is little consciousness of walking with him as a friend and knowing him as the one who really cares. They *talk* about this aspect of Jesus, but in reality he is for them a legalistic Lord, and God is the Judge of the universe. If they should ever really consider God as their Father or Jesus as the compassionate and loving Savior, these concepts would create a revolution in their lives. These stern Christians do not live out the meaning of grace, even though they talk about it all the time.

We are always fighting on two fronts. On the one side are the softies who do not see Christ as Lord, and on the other the Pharisees who do not see Christ as merciful. On the one side are the guilty who can never accept forgiveness for their sins, and on the other the guiltless who never think of their sins at all. Some think of Jesus strictly as God without any real humanity, and others see him only as a man, but not as the only begotten Son of God. We fight on both fronts. But why must it be either/or? Why cannot Christ be both God and man, both Judge and merciful?

Even more disquieting is the fact that some dismiss the words of Jesus altogether! They prefer to receive Christianity from the letters of Paul. The charge that Protestantism has become Pauline may have some truth in it after all. Paul was a great man and his writing is inspired Scripture. Every part of Scripture is given by inspiration of God and that includes the Old Testament as well. I am not insisting that the Gospels must be more important than the letters of Paul; yet they can hardly be less significant either. After all, Paul was not the Savior of the world.

Years ago the critics attacked Protestantism with the charge that it had moved away from a simple belief in Jesus to the complicated dogmatic system of Paul, from the Gospels to the epistles. This nineteenth-century barrage was actually a revolt against the person of Christ, with the first move against one of his principal spokesmen. Everything they disliked about Christianity was attributed to Paul. The truth is that the teachings of Paul can be traced to the words of Jesus, such as his emphasis on justification by faith, the resurrection, and the judgment.

In spite of these unwarranted charges, evangelicals have seldom actively reversed the trend. Ministers preach more sermons from Paul than Jesus. Whenever a group of Christians meet for Bible study or attend a conference, they usually study one of the letters of Paul. People are quite surprised if the words of Jesus are suggested in place of that more familiar terrain.

On top of all this, a teaching labeled "dispensationalism" continues within the Church. It is based on statements from the Bible—certainly not complete falsehoods—which imply that God treats man in varying ways depending on the dispensation (the age) in which he lives. The most obvious of the differences is the division between the Old and the New Testaments. Under the Old, God gave man the law and expected him to obey it. In the New, God rewards man according to his mercy in Christ, not through the law: "The law was given by Moses, but grace and truth came by Jesus Christ."[3]

So there is a dispensation of law and a dispensation of grace. This system of interpretation, however, tends to overlook the truth that God has always accepted man through faith and never because of other qualifications.[4] But the real damage is inflicted when it comes to the words of Jesus. They are interpreted *under the Old* instead of as initiating the New. Hence only that which follows the death and resurrection of Christ is for the Church. For whom then are the words of Jesus? For the Jews! They have no bearing on Christians. Thus, in one stroke, are wiped out the teachings of our Lord.

I have been struck with this twisted interpretation as I have taught the words of Jesus to several groups. What would seem obvious in the parables is twisted so that the applications are for the disciples under the old dispensation, and have no meaning for us. "The kingdom of heaven is like unto treasure hid in a field; the which when a man has found, he hides, and for joy thereof goes and sells all that he has, and buys that field."[5] What is this treasure? In dispensational teaching, *Jesus* is interpreted to be the man who sells everything to obtain the treasure. He leaves heaven, comes to earth, and dies on the cross to obtain the treasure. What is the treasure? "Israel," they say. You take that all in and when you get through with this razzle-dazzle you ask: "So what? What has this to say to me? Very interesting, but I couldn't care less."

In reality this parable is an explanation of what has been happening in Jesus' ministry. He has brought God's word to man. Some have rejected it, others have treated it casually, some have given it a listen. He, the sower of the seed, has observed a varied response. Some have let it go in one ear and out the other, and others have truly responded. But what is this seed, this word of God? It is really a treasure! It is worth *everything!* And he who sees it as such will sell everything he has to obtain it. The kingdom of God which Jesus proclaims is that treasure.

That interpretation has meaning for us. For it raises questions: "What do you think of the kingdom of God? What is it worth to you? How much will you give to obtain it?" *These* haunting questions can never be dismissed by a casual "So what?"

Similarly the Sermon on the Mount is scratched. (Is it any wonder we need a new look at Jesus?) Such easy disposal is so terribly convenient, for the Sermon on the Mount is difficult to interpret, let alone apply to everyday living. And since it is so impossible anyway, I'm perfectly right in removing it from my list. Then I won't have to try to live that way, for I'm justified by faith. So I need only Paul for my religion—not Jesus.

How dare we remove Jesus and the Incarnation—the coming of God into human flesh? How dare we strike out God's message to man in word and deed, in teaching and event? For this is God speaking—not just to the Jews under the old dispensation, but to the world, to every man, to all his creation. Jesus lived life as it ought to be lived, and all Scripture is the interpretation of that event. Even Paul would be aghast at the dichotomy we have created. He wrote: "Let Christ himself be your example as to what your attitude should be."[6] He urged us to have the mind of Christ.

How can the mind of Jesus be in you unless you listen to his teaching? How can you have the mind of humility apart from coming to him who is lowly in heart? Then, what did he say to us? What did he teach? What about the parables, the Sermon on the Mount and all the rest of it? Obviously you can't throw it away by misinterpretation or misrepresentation. All Christian thought must not only find its roots in Jesus' teaching, but needs to be led back to the event of the Son of Man.

"The Sermon on the Mount is more a statement of what will happen to a man when he allows Jesus to get hold of him, than a statement of what a man must do if he is to follow Jesus. . . . Thus the Sermon on the Mount is seen to be not a code of conduct given to men to follow, but a statement of issues which receive their ultimate validity, meaning and relevance only as they are recognized to be issues raised by Christ."[7]

What we are really talking about is the importance of Jesus to Christianity. Of course all Christians admit that he is important, but the question is, in what way? To some Jesus is important because of his death and resurrection. To others because of his birth, miracles and coming again. To others for his teaching and contributions to our world. (We find ourselves again fighting on two fronts!) Those who regard Jesus of value for his *deeds* need to consider the impact of his *words*. Those who care only about his teaching must open their eyes to his sacrificial death and triumphant resurrection.

What he said was significant because of who he was; he spoke the word of God. And what he was to accomplish had great worth to him: "The Son of man came . . . to give his life a ransom for many."[8] Neither of these facets can be avoided. If we only take out some aspects of the good news which may please us, we will turn out to be pagan evangelicals who know all the labels of our doctrines, without knowing Christ's actual word to us. On the other hand we may turn out to be pagan liberals who try to follow Christ's teaching without accepting his atoning work through which alone we may taste the forgiveness of sins.

A partial Christianity which refuses to take seriously every aspect of both Christ's work and his words is like taking the field in a ball game without a center fielder or a shortstop. It could be done, of course, but balls hit in either direction are sure to give all kinds of trouble. And who would think of giving this advantage to the opposition in a world series game?

This is exactly what we are doing in partial Christianity. If Jesus is God in human flesh—and we Christians believe this—then how can we divorce his deeds from our thought? How can we separate his teaching from our life? *Everything* in Christ is like treasure, for he is that treasure. The lack of Christlike living in the Church is not due to our insincerity or conscious hypocrisy. It is simply our failure to listen to Jesus, to ponder his words and apply them—to be, as our name implies, little Christs. How far we are from anything like this needs hardly to be affirmed, for we are quite conscious of it. When Paul instructs us to "copy me as I copy Christ,"[9] he not only throws the weight of his teaching behind Jesus, but urges us to live our lives in imitation of Christ.

To copy Christ, what does this mean? Imitating him? Is that a legitimate word still today as it was years ago? Imitation ice cream may taste fairly good, but it is *not* ice cream. Well, we are not the real thing either; we are not Christ. And yet there is more to it than putting it in the negative. Copying Christ means a desire to look up and away from ourselves. It means a willingness to listen to him and do what he says. By humbly learning from him we confess that we really believe his way of life to be superior to our own.

But here comes the snag: Do we believe this? Not really! We believe our own way is better. That's why the Sermon on the Mount gets so much static from us. It may be all right for Jesus, we say, but does he really expect us to obey him? Surely not that!

What would happen if we believed this to be God's word to us? What if we believed we were to copy him, as Paul also says? What changes this would make. How we are to interpret the Sermon on the Mount is not the issue. How we are to follow Christ is also another matter. Are we willing to *listen?*

Are we convinced that we ought to *live* by his revealed word? These are the important questions. For, after all, Jesus himself tells us that to apply his teaching is our wisdom, and to fail to do so is foolishness.[10]

Therefore a renewed urging to imitate Jesus is not what is needed. Everything really depends on our attitude, our point of view. Are we self-sufficient blockheads willing to acknowledge that his is a better way of life? Are we self-centered goody-goodies willing to take Jesus as our Savior and Lord, in every sense of those words? And does that not mean that we also walk with him as our Friend and listen to him as our Teacher?

This word "teacher" has been eliminated from the language of many Christians simply because it does not say enough about Jesus. Of course it does not say enough. Jesus is more than a teacher; he is the unique Son of God, the eternal Word made flesh. So why even bring up this inferior word "teacher"? Nicodemus used the word to refer to Jesus: "You are a teacher come from God."[11] And he was told he had to be born again.

Perhaps the word "teacher" was buried beneath the soil of greater titles because it was used by people who were not Christians. But to acknowledge Jesus as our Teacher does not limit him to this title. I want to resurrect it, at least long enough for our consideration, since it ought not to have died. It seems that Jesus was pleased that Nicodemus recognized him as a Teacher come from God. No other Pharisees had approached him in this way. He accepted the title graciously.

Perhaps it was because of this title that Jesus went on to teach Nicodemus about new birth. As a Teacher come from God his authority to speak was acknowledged by Nicodemus. Had Nicodemus not said this much, would Jesus have replied in the same forthright manner? Perhaps not.

Nicodemus was quite right. Jesus is our Teacher come from God, and not to listen to him would be a crime of major proportions. Evangelical Christians will only be saved from the doldrums when we make a sincere attempt to listen to Jesus and begin to do what he says. Copying Christ is not a convenient extra. Every Christian needs earnestly to pursue the mind of Christ.

In the parable of the sower Jesus himself illustrates what happens when we receive his word. His teaching is like seed which carries the potential of life. When it enters into a man's thinking, like seed in soil, it will bring forth a good harvest. Of course the right conditions must prevail. The soul (like the soil) must be prepared, made ready to receive the word. The more the word is allowed to enter, and the more time it is given to grow, the better the crop will be. For one thing, Christians need to learn that we have only so much time and so much room and so much potential. If the teaching of Christ is not given prominence, other and lesser matters will take over.

At the Julier Pass in Switzerland eight thousand feet above sea level, a shepherd experienced a sudden snowstorm. His sheep became terrified and ran wildly in all directions. Amid the driving snow they could not see the dangerous abyss and many fell to their deaths. At this the shepherd climbed a rock and began to shout. Those sheep who heard his voice came running and gathered around him. Thus they were rescued.

Only those from the flock of Christ who in our time are able to hear the word of our good Shepherd will be rescued from a life of empty beliefs to meaning and purpose. Our discovery of God depends on our discovery of Jesus. He calls us "o'er the tumult Of our life's wild, restless sea; Day by day his sweet voice soundeth, Saying, 'Christian, follow me.' "[13]

Has the time not come for us to take a new look at Jesus?

NOTES:

1. Pierre Berton, *The Comfortable Pew* (Philadelphia: J. B. Lippincott Company, 1965), p. 83.
2. See my book *Jesus, The Revolutionary* (Glendale, Calif.: Regal Books, 1966), especially the chapters on The Revolutionary, The Fearless, and the Disturbing Christ.
3. John 1:17.

4. See Rom. 4:1–16.
5. Matt. 13:44.
6. Phil. 2:5 (Phillips).
7. Daniel T. Niles, *That They May Have Life* (New York: Harper & Row, Inc., 1951), pp. 47, 49.
8. Matt. 20:28.
9. I Cor. 11:1 (Phillips).
10. See Matt. 7:24–27.
11. John 3:2.
12. Matt. 13:1–23.
13. C. F. Alexander.

24.

The Art of Communication

ONE of my frustrations has been to say things about Christianity in language which can be understood by anyone interested without being misunderstood by Christians. It is, however, difficult to communicate concepts and ideas which cannot always be conveyed through ordinary language. (How can one really write about love?) Those who produce oversimplified books lose the actual truths of Christianity, and those who are overly technical or theological never reach the common man.

Jesus was able to speak the truth in such simple language. He never employed any of the involved theological gobbledygook which is so often Christian talk. Did Jesus *ever* talk about "sanctification," "glorification," "incarnation," "trinity," or "eschatology"? Did he ever suggest to anyone that they should be "under the blood"? Did he ever talk about "being relevantly related to the existential situation?" Did he use the cant phrases of which some are so fond? To the contrary. Jesus talked about water, bread, wine, trees, mountains, birds, flowers, fish, money, home, pearls, roads, and light. He used such simple words that we cannot forget the truths he hung on them. He certainly never tried to impress anyone.

In a world where East and West do not understand each other and where an increase in divorce illustrates the breakdown of communication between husbands and wives, Christians are not able to make themselves plainly understood either. And yet the task of every minister is communication. If he cannot simplify his language, he is really most inadequate. Why should any minister desire to be more complicated than Jesus? If he cannot make himself understood, he misses the whole point of his ministry.

If a minister starts talking about a balm in Gilead, he need not be surprised if some begin to wonder where the bomb is planted? How dangerous is it? Or is he speaking about a bum? Where in the world is this bum? Where is Gilead anyway? How many people understand this to be an expression of healing and comfort from the Bible? The fault lies not merely in the pronunciation (balm, bum, bomb), but in the use of an unfamiliar figure of speech without clarification.

Among his many pastoral responsibilities the minister must communicate the great truths of Christianity. No matter how well he may do in every other task, the failure of the American church lies particularly with the minister's inability to communicate meaningfully and enthusiastically.

We ministers do not communicate meaningfully, because we do not spend sufficient time in the study. Most ministers I know do their reading on the run. The pastorate is such a hectic affair with its many varied duties, that the average minister is continually administrating, committeeing, visiting, or running around. He is hardly ever at his desk. Rare is the man who can block off two or three hours a day for study and preparation of sermons. Consequently sermons are rather like a hash blended together in a few spare moments with little more flavor than what comes right out of the can. They are pre-cooked and served without any time spent. Even an occasional joke or story from *The Readers' Digest* doesn't do much for it.

"A poem is never a put-up job," said Robert Frost. "It begins as a lump in the throat, a sense of wrong, a homesickness, a lovesickness." How much more must that be true for communicating eternal truth? Whether or not we are able to produce a true poem every week, ministers need far more labor and heart bestowed on our sermons. Or else we will be preaching Jericho sermons, marching around the subject seven times like the children of Israel, and making lots of noise. Perhaps some walls will come tumbling down, but the listeners will be no better off than the inhabitants of Jericho who didn't know what was going on either.

We are not enthusiastically communicating because we are no longer convinced about the joy of preaching nor its effectiveness. Preaching, we say, doesn't really change anyone. We have the notion that small groups or personal counseling achieve more. They help people. (The Church has been very much influenced by the psychological approach.) There is nothing wrong with such methods, but they should not drive preaching into the shadows. Preaching did change people in the past, and the liveliest congregations today are generally those around an enthusiastic and realistic communicator of the faith.

Of course if the sermon is just a rehash of the week's events or even a dry Bible study, nothing will ever happen. Those who lack enthusiasm can never be contagious, nor are they convinced themselves! Our lack of enthusiasm is due to our contentment in the shallow waters, without getting the feel of all that lies beyond in truth and reality. And if a minister shuns the deep water, how can he expect the congregation to wade in further?

It may sound strange to accuse a busy person of laziness. And yet if a preacher refuses to gain insight into Christianity, to study, read, and look afresh at Jesus Christ, could all his activity be an attempt to keep from study and prayer? It is *hard* to study the Bible and then make it applicable to life. It can never be done by repeating the old phrases, for these orthodox words will be swallowed by the people familiar with them, swallowed whole and pass through undigested. And that may eventually cause spiritual pain. We must be contemporary.

A lukewarm drip from the pulpit makes nobody angry, and no one says, "This is meant for me." People simply walk out without being touched. They protest nothing and remain unmoved. They smile and coo, "I enjoyed that sermon." Meanwhile, back in the church, the minister congratulates himself on making out so well after so hectic a week, and tells himself that he is really doing a bang-up job. Such smugness and self-satisfaction may sound unbelievable, but they exist and help to strengthen the preacher's self-protecting armor.

A different factor has affected the pew. We live in an advertising era which so overstates every product that we don't know what to believe any more. What is really trustworthy? A politician may deliver a magnificently convincing speech, but how many words are contrived to get votes? If afterwards, in a back room, he turns to a close friend and adds, "Now, if you want to hear my personal opinion . . . ," how can anyone trust him? Who believes all that jargon on television about the soaps which wash the whitest white? Is every toothpaste the greatest? And which filter really filters out the nicotine? No wonder we are confused. And all of it is offered with enthusiasm, sometimes even passion. A spiritless minister stands in pale comparison with the splash for aspirin. No wonder an anemic presentation of Christianity is dismissed by the pew which has its emotions charged elsewhere twenty times a day.

There are others in the pews of evangelical churches who are actually on the lookout for all the orthodox phrases. They will not give a man a hearing until they have heard him use the right words. It is devastating to think that a man may be under continual surveillance and be actually tuned out by the listeners, until he has declared, by the proper phraseology, that he believes in those fundamentals which make him orthodox.

But if the communication between pastor and people remains an enigma, even more does the communication between Christians and our secular society. The Church is the only organization in the world which exists primarily for those who are not its members. This is why we take the obligation of communication so seriously. We do not live in the Roman era, nor in Medieval times or the Renaissance. We are no longer in the Victorian nineteenth century but in the scientific, secular and materialistic era of the twentieth century. We must speak to our age.

"We are secular in the sense that we pursue the immediate

goals of life, without asking too many questions about the meaning of life. Secularism dismisses ultimate questions about the meaning of existence, partly because it believes that science has answered these questions and partly because it regards the questions as unanswerable or uninteresting." (Certainly a devastating comment on our times!) "Materialism is the pursuit, not of happiness, but of comfort and physical security."[1]

Has not the pursuit of this-world-comfort become a substitute for any ultimate questions about another world for twentieth-century man? Why are we satisfied only with the immediate questions and why have we dismissed all questions of eternal value? Why do we seek freedom *from* religion rather than freedom *in* religion?

J. B. Priestley comes to this conclusion in a penetrating survey of Western man: "Any last pretence of society having a religious foundation and framework, being contained at all by religion, has vanished. Patterns of living that had existed for thousands of years are destroyed within a generation. . . . In this atomic age we are sure of nothing but sex, and we are now piling on to sex the whole gigantic load of our increasing dissatisfactions, our despair, a burden far greater than it can safely take. . . . Religion alone can carry the load, defend us against the dehumanizing collectives, restore true personality."[2]

The Christian faces a culture that has ceased to be religion-based for the first time in Western civilization. How then can we communicate with this world? How can we emphasize those things which are eternal but which disturb the patterns of living? How can we raise questions which have been rejected by modern man as meaningful? How can this seemingly impossible gulf be spanned?

One of the classic answers of Christians has been withdrawal. We have withdrawn from the task. There is too much clash and conflict and so we retreat (as Christians in another era retreated behind monastery walls) within our separated groups to enjoy our religion exclusively for ourselves. Evangelicals have tended to hide behind their church walls, pulling the doors shut after them, to enjoy "Christian fellowship." *The world is so rotten, let it go to hell. Christ will come back soon; therefore there is no need to get concerned in and for our world. We can't change it anyway.*

And for all this we have a Scripture: "Come out from among them and be ye separate, saith the Lord."[3] We do not want to open our eyes to see that our application is actually a flagrant misuse of that particular verse; it does not sanction withdrawal. To come out from among them does not mean retreating from our culture; it means not living for the same goals as secular man. Jesus never withdrew from weddings or parties, but he was separated in his heart. That is, he had different values, he was concerned with more than a this-world outlook.

What happens when Christians adopt the other-world policy? By withdrawing from education they allow the world to become totally pragmatic and scholastic, so that spiritual emphases are hardly to be found anywhere. By withdrawing from politics, they allow other points of view to take over. By their withdrawal from literature, books become increasingly sexy, secular, solutionless. The same emptiness may be observed in business, philosophy, sociology, psychology, science, art. Instead of becoming Christian educators, Christian writers, Christian businessmen, Christian leaders, we leave it to non-Christian Joe. But, then we cannot blame Joe if the results are not what we could wish—only ourselves.

"I do not believe (I am a Christian myself) that the culture could survive the complete disappearance of the Christian faith. . . . If Christianity goes the whole of our culture goes," says T. S. Eliot.[4]

Other Christians have accommodated themselves. They have allowed themselves to be absorbed by the culture, with the result that the Church and the world have become one—almost indistinguishable. What happens then? Then the prophetic voice is heard no longer. Then Christians cannot stand over against the world.

This has happened in our own country. Absorbed in the American way of life, we have identified the American way of life with Christianity. As Christians we enrich the culture by adding comfort and peace, which is like adding coloring to lemonade. Making it pink pretties it up, but does nothing to the taste. And, if the American way is the lemonade to which Christianity adds the coloring, it will not be long before Christianity is totally out. It serves no *useful* function!

Since the world wants Christianity to be no more than the flavor in *its* lemonade, wants Christianity only for the invocations of secular events, wants to pursue its own ends and enjoy its own policies, any voice lifted against it will be quenched. This is so because "the whole godless world lies in the power of the evil one."[5]

Neither of these two solutions are workable. The Christian cannot withdraw, nor can he allow himself to be absorbed. He must be able to communicate to his world in meaningful ways about reality and life. How can he do this? "The business of the Church (is) to say what is wrong . . . morally wrong that is, what is inconsistent with Christian doctrine . . . and why it is wrong. . . . Perhaps the dominant vice of our time, from the point of view of the Church, will be proved to be avarice. Surely there is something wrong in our attitude towards money. The acquisitive rather than the creative and spiritual instincts are encouraged (in the secular society). . . . The Church has perpetually to answer this question: to what purpose were we born? What is the end of man?"[6]

Perhaps we can also point out that this secular age which dismisses ultimate questions, is still most superstitious. Over three thousand newspapers print astrology forecasts. A radio syndicate offers hourly advice to its listeners from a famous astrologer. Millions of people who have with sophistication overthrown the supernatural, believe that their behavior is determined by the signs of the Zodiac. The stars in the heavens arrange their lives for them, not from the secular age but from *out there!* A culture which leaves God out settles for substitutes. Why should we not turn back from the false to the true and living God?

Not until we understand the human dilemma are we able to speak to anyone. How can we come running with the answers until we have heard the questions? Unless we listen first, we will make the kind of mistake that appeared in the first printing of a new hymnal, when a hymn for funerals was misplaced in the section for weddings. It began: "Go happy soul, thy days are ended!" Christians have often failed to communicate because they have quickly jumped to conclusions. An opportunity to be heard will always be given to the person who has first opened channels of communication through listening.

Although essentially we communicate a fact ("God was in Christ"),[7] we can only communicate it through life and language. Language apart from life is hollow, empty talk. Mere words, even if they are the right words, fail to convince the world. But a life apart from words about Christ glorifies the self: "I am such a good person. See how much good I do—for you." The cup of cold water is given *in Jesus' name,* and this is the only harmony of faith and works which effectively shares the good news.

"Communication of the message is the crowning category of which all activities of the Church in evangelizing, preaching, teaching, and witnessing to all fields of life are part. It is also a task that must constantly be restarted. There is no part of life, nor of the world, which is ever definitely evangelized."[8]

God has talked with us not only in shouting his laws from a mountain or through his prophets, but when he came personally into our midst. We Christians have always believed this to be the highest type of communication: Christ, the Word of God, the Eternal made temporal, the distant God come near, drawn into the miseries of this life. Not only is this the message, but it is also the method of communication. As Christ came into the world, so the Church is to enter the world on his behalf. This is what he told us: "As my Father has sent me, even so send I you."[9]

Now that we have realized our need for confession, awareness and honesty, and have emphasized the place of the Bible, the need for communication and the new look at Jesus, I am only concerned about one other factor before we turn to a composite picture of a Christian.

Humorist Bennett Cerf tells the story of a new lighthouse

which was erected on a dangerous shore in the Northwest. A couple of Eskimos watched every detail of the construction, and when the lighthouse began to function, they were on hand to watch operations. Then one night a heavy fog blew in. One of the Eskimos triumphantly turned to the other and said: "I told you white igloo builder no good. Light shine, bell ding-dong, horn woo-woo, but fog come rolling in just the same."[10]

Now that we have thought through what is wrong with the Church, will we do anything about it? Anything constructive? Or will the same fog roll in again, obscuring our vision of God, keeping us from action?

"Where there is no vision, the people perish."[11]

NOTES:

1. Reinhold Niebuhr, *Pious and Secular America* (New York: Charles Scribner's Sons, 1958), pp. 2,3.
2. J. B. Priestly, *Literature and Western Man* (New York: Harper & Row, Inc., 1960), pp. 442–444.
3. II Cor. 6:17.
4. T. S. Eliot, *Christianity and Culture* (New York: Harcourt, Brace & World, 1949), p. 200.
5. I John 5:19, *New English Bible.*
6. T. S. Eliot, *op. cit.,* pp. 74–77.
7. II Cor. 5:19.
8. Hendrik Kraemer, *The Communication of the Christian Faith* (Philadelphia: The Westminster Press, 1956), p. 23. Copyright, 1956, W. L. Jenkins, The Westminster Press. Used by permission.
9. John 20:29.
10. Bennett Cerf in *The Life of the Party* (New York: Doubleday & Company, 1956). Copyright © 1956 by Bennett Cerf. Reprinted by permission of Doubleday & Co. Inc.
11. Prov. 29:18.

25.

What, Then, Is a Christian?

SOME years ago while counseling junior high boys at camp, I asked them on the first night: "How would you define a Christian? What would you say a Christian is?" These boys had been brought up in Protestant churches and reflected their Sunday school training and their parents' thinking. These were their answers:

"A Christian is an American."

"I think," said another after mulling the question over a bit, "that a Christian is a man who does good and lives by the golden rule."

"A Christian is a person who goes to church," added a third.

"A Christian is someone who believes in the Lord."

None of these replies were satisfactory, nor do they define a Christian compositely. To identify a Christian with an American is to subscribe to the heresy of Israel when they claimed to be the exclusive people of God—nobody else qualified. To identify a Christian with a person who does good and lives by the golden rule makes no distinction between a Christian, a Buddhist, a Mohammedan or any moral man. Many who attend church are not necessarily Christians, just as a wheelbarrow does not become a car simply by putting it in the garage.

And to believe in the Lord raises the question, "Which Lord? Allah? Krishna? Yahweh?"

Is it really possible to define a Christian apart from Jesus Christ?

A Christian is one who follows Jesus Christ. He believes in Christ as his Savior and trusts him as his Lord. He freely commits his life out of gratitude since he belongs to the Crucified who suffered in his stead. A Christian is not a person who points to himself, declaring: "I am a Christian." He is rather a person who points away from himself, confessing: "I believe in Jesus Christ." A Christian is a person who has entered into a relationship with God as his Father. He is a Christian not due to a subjective experience alone, but because of objective facts. He does not trust in his experience but in Christ. He does not rely on an emotional moment by which he was born into the new life; he was born *of God* and therefore believes God who has made all things new.

God came into the world in Jesus Christ. Christ gave his life for the world and triumphed over death. In these objective realities a Christian sees the love of God. He bases his salvation not on what he may have achieved, but on what he has received from this merciful God.

"Many a time I have heard people discussing Christianity, criticizing, approving, patronizing it—apparently under the impression that Christianity is a compendium of ethical advice, an ideology, a philosophy of life, an amalgam of certain specialized virtues. . . . Jesus does not claim, with the founders of certain ethnic religions, to suggest answers to the world's enigmas; He claims to *be* the answer. . . . He does not offer the guidance of a code or a philosophy to keep men right through the uncertainties of an unknown future. . . . As Kierkegaard expressed it: 'All other religions are oblique; the founder stands aside and introduces another speaker; they themselves therefore come under religion—Christianity alone is direct speech.' "[1]

We live in a world where Jesus Christ is the risen, living Lord, and therefore inescapable. To believe in this Christ is to be grasped by his presence, to move in the certainty that we are not alone: "All power is given unto me in heaven and in earth. . . . Lo, I am with you alway, even unto the end of the world."[2] Unless we believe not only that Jesus *lived* but that he *lives,* unless we bring the weight of the Christian faith to bear upon our present life, we can hardly call ourselves Christians. Believing facts from the past is not equivalent to being an awakened and dedicated disciple.

In the Second World War a paratrooper said that the first time he had to leap out of his plane, everything in him resisted. He had heard all the lectures, mastered the techniques of using the ropes, practiced jumping under simulated conditions, but when it came right down to jumping from the plane, he could not believe as he sped through the air that this frail piece of cloth would actually hold him up. Then came the moment and "nothing in this world compares with the thrill I experienced when I leaped into the sky, pulled the cord and found that the whole thing was actually true, that the parachute would support me and take me safely to the ground."

Christianity is *not* a parachute by which we float through this world in safety. It may even be that our faith is more frail than a parachute. You can't feel it, touch it, see it. But we will never master Christianity by book study or by simulation, only by a plunge of faith and willingness to follow Jesus Christ. Follow him as you understand him now! Come to him as you are. Learn of him, put him to the test, but begin where you are.

This, then, is reality for us. Christ is God in human flesh. He died in our place. He rose from the dead and is alive forevermore. He is with us now. He will judge the world.

A rebroadcast of a news event is hardly of interest, particularly if you know how it will turn out. Viewing a space trip at the moment of take off is exciting, but a tape of what happened yesterday has lost immediateness. Is that the problem with our Christian faith? Must we recapture the long ago and far away, or can we live on the edge of reality because Christ is here now? *Now!*

This was the one thing which the book *In His Steps* had going for it. Millions read it because the question, "What would Jesus do?" was applied in the present tense. The author placed Jesus into everyday, concrete situations. And people soon discovered that they had to know Jesus before they could even ask the question of what he would do. They had to study him, learn from him, come into his presence to feel his influence and receive his guidance. A number of the characters in the book attempted to live the Christ-life and, in spite of ridicule from many quarters, persevered. Who raises such questions today? Are they legitimate questions? I believe they are. What would Jesus have us to do? Will not asking this question give us personal guidance, an impetus for social action and missionary concern? And if Christ is alive as we affirm, can we not find his direction through meditative prayer and faith?

Unfortunately, the emphasis on contemplation has vanished from the evangelical landscape, to our great loss. We talk about devotions, but they have become so mechanical that we never approach the depths through reflective thought on the word of God. We simply don't make time for anything that demands something from us. Because the Christian who draws upon the life of Christ daily is confronted with the necessity of letting down the barriers which keep Christ out of his life?

Think of the disciplines Jesus spoke about: "If your right eye leads you astray pluck it out and throw it away; it is better for you to lose one of your members than that your whole body should be thrown on to the rubbish heap. Yes, if your right hand leads you astray cut it off and throw it away; it is better for you to lose one of your members than that your whole body should go to the rubbish heap."[3] Gouge out an eye? Cut off a hand? This cannot be taken literally of course, or else all Christians would lose not only their sight in less than two weeks, but their hands, feet, ears, tongues and other members. Obviously no one interprets these verses literally, nor ought we. On the other hand, who takes Christianity seriously enough to deal effectively with his sins?

Martin Luther remarked so many times that we all sin every day. In his Larger Catechism he affirms that "we sin daily in words and deeds, by commission and omission" and in the Smaller Catechism adds that we "deserve only punishment."

Luther presents no idealized picture of the Christian life. We are sinners till our dying day, struggling with the temptations of the flesh, beggars of the grace of God. And yet we must be careful not to misunderstand his emphasis.

> What Luther himself meant is plain from the whole tenor of his life and teaching. Much of his thought was determined by that against which he was reacting. He was determined that there should be no trace left of any righteousness of man's own, of any smallest rag of virtue, on which man could base any claim to stand on his own merits in the presence of God. At the same time he was determined to make clear that "sanctification" is not something that man can work out in his own strength, and that might produce in him afresh a sense of independence over against God. But neither of these attitudes prevented him from filling his sermons with vigorous ethical and practical counsels, or from making plain that to live in Christ must involve radical consequences in the plain everyday world of practical goodness and virtue.[4]

This balance is needed by Christians. A Christian is a sinner who is nevertheless told to live in the flesh and above his sins. The promise of the Christian life is not that we shall not ever sin, but that, recognizing evil for what it is, we may live victoriously in Christ. The seed of sin which consists of a disobedient will is removed: "The man who is really God's son does not practice sin, for God's nature is in him, for good, and such a heredity is incapable of sin."[5]

The actual sins that such a person commits are not an expression of that person's true desires. He is not motivated by his sinful nature, but he may still yield to sin: "If we refuse to admit that we are sinners, then we live in a world of illusion and truth becomes a stranger to us. But if we freely admit that we have sinned, we find God utterly reliable and straightforward—he forgives our sins and makes us thoroughly clean from all that is evil."[6]

It should now become clear that Christianity offers not an idealized picture but the rugged reality of learning to live in forgiveness and love, in spite of continuing failures. Such a view could make it easy for us to become pessimists. But a Christian is also an optimist, or at least a man of hope, when he appropriates God's ever-present mercy, receives the forgiveness that comes from above, and basks in the acceptance of Christ himself. The important thing for the Christian life is not simply the pursuit of holiness, but the ability to live daily in the free grace of God. If we had only the goal of holiness before us, we would finally give up in despair. As sinners who remain sinners however, we are always recipients of his love.

"Christianity is strange. It bids man recognise that he is vile, even abominable, and bids him desire to be like God. Without such a counterpoise, this dignity would make him horribly vain, or this humiliation would make him terribly abject."[7] Christian faith acknowledges human weakness without falling into despair, and human greatness without falling into pride.

I need all the help I can get to live the Christian life. I need the fellowship of Christians, the practice of contemplation and devotion, the opportunities of service, the Spirit of the living God, the attendance at Communion, the assurance that a fellow Christian accepts me with all my weaknesses. I need to believe in a Love which seeks me and a Power available for me in all my daily struggles.

Above all, a Christian is a person who is not bound by rules and regulations so that he lives under a burden of "thou shalts" and "thou shalt nots." Rather, he is a person who, according to the words of Jesus, has been set free. "If the Son therefore shall make you free, ye shall be free indeed."[8] This freedom has come through the removal of his sins and his being accepted by Jesus Christ. Too many of us talk about accepting Christ and never about his accepting us. For us to accept his atonement for our sins is one side of the coin. He also accepts us as his disciples and followers, even as the Father receives his straying son when he comes back home. To live in this acceptance is to live in freedom. To know we belong in his family because he does not reject us and tells us this good news is to breathe the air of joy.

Dietrich Bonhoeffer has an important word for us Christians: "The Christian is the man who no longer seeks his salvation, his deliverance, his justification in himself, but in Jesus Christ alone. He knows that God's Word in Jesus Christ pronounces him guilty, even when he does not feel his guilt, and God's Word in Jesus Christ pronounces him not guilty and righteous, even when he does not feel that he is righteous at all. The Christian . . . lives wholly by God's word pronounced upon him. . . ."[9]

What Bonhoeffer is saying is that a Christian does not live simply by feeling. He may in fact not feel his guilt, but he is guilty nevertheless; or his righteousness, but he is pronounced righteous in Christ! By this objective word he lives; amid these heavenly shadows he learns to rest securely. We live in a tension of life and death, happiness and renunciation, achievement and humility, guilt and righteousness. This does not mean we are not Christians, but it does mean we start being honest about our conflict. This is the reality of the Christian man.

"Well, let's now at any rate come clean. Prayer *is* irksome. An excuse to omit it is never unwelcome. When it is over, this casts a feeling of relief and holiday over the rest of the day. We are reluctant to begin. We are delighted to finish. While we are at prayer, but not while we are reading a novel or solving a cross-word puzzle, any trifle is enough to distract us."[10]

So writes one of the greatest apologists for Christianity, a man who was a devoted Christian for many years, in what turned out to be his last book! Even when prayer went well yesterday, he adds, today it may again be a burden. "If I were a Calvinist this symptom would fill me with despair." (Is this why many Calvinists are loathe to discuss what is going on in their inner lives?) Mr. Lewis then says that this paradox exists to be transcended, that is, to be overcome. How?

"As practical imperatives for here and now the two great commandments have to be translated 'Behave *as if* you loved God and man.' For no man can love because he is told to. . . . And if a man really loved God and man, once again this would hardly be obedience; for if he did, he would be unable to help it. Thus the command really says to us, 'Ye must be born again.' "[11] Obviously this is a life-long calling, during which we learn that only through God can we love God.

It would not destroy Christianity to admit that there are some ethical pagans who have attained higher moral standards than some Christians. In fact, being a Christian has not made untidy persons tidy, or people who are never on time punctual. There are sincere Christians who suffer from impatience, irritability, anxiety, or unclean thoughts.

Now this does not mean we should give up the ship. Christianity must be lived to be understood, and understanding it will help us in living. It must be lived in all its seeming paradox by us as redeemed sinners. The New Testament does not set forth a full-blown theological system which must be accepted in its entirety before you can call yourself a Christian, nor must you reach perfection before you can even call yourself one. Jesus invites us to follow him and share in this pilgrimage in spite of any obstacles we will meet.

To follow Jesus will mean one thing to one and something else to another. Some will work for social justice, others will serve humbly in their homes. Some will enter politics, education, law, or the arts, whereas others will simply give a cup of cold water in Jesus' name. And yet every Christian will show forth a faith in action.

Throwing in the towel because we cannot meet any standards is all too easy. If the goal were not to be like Christ, who would attempt anything? We would merely sink into the muck of our own contentment. The attempt for sainthood—which is not an attempt to find out what *I* can become, but rather what God can do through me—is not in vain. "What we shall be has not yet been disclosed, but we know that when it is disclosed we shall be like him, because we shall see him as he is."[12] The greatest work in the world is to approach our destiny. What more compelling pull can a human being experience?

Mahatma Gandhi once made this suggestion to a Christian group: "I would suggest, first, that all of you Christians begin to live more like Jesus Christ. Second, I would suggest that you practice your religion without toning it down. Third, I would suggest that you put your emphasis on love, for love is the center and soul of Christianity."[13]

How? By believing God utterly, by loving him sincerely, and by serving man gladly. All this becomes a reality through the Holy Spirit, not through our own achievements. A Christian is a person who receives this Spirit from above, the motivation and power within. "With the help of the Holy Spirit, the animal nature can be curbed, chained, subdued, mastered. No more of it need be admitted to my moral life than fellowship with God in Christ allows. . . . So long as life is truly lived in God, I am further forward and the temptation weakens. . . . In the power of the Holy Spirit it grows easier with passing time."[14] The energy of the Spirit is available to all Christians.

No, being a Christian does not solve all problems, either intellectual or moral; but even as a tree spreads out its roots in the direction of the prevailing wind to strengthen itself against the storm, so Christians can learn to dig in. Especially if they are planted by the rivers of water.[15] For Christ is not someone I lean on as a crutch in times of difficulty, but rather the very soil into which I put my roots, the ground on which I stand.

A Christian, then, is a person who stands in need of the grace of God, who lives by faith in Jesus Christ, who is free and responsible, accepted as well as striving, loved as well as loving. Most of all, he is one who suffers. He suffers because he has been died for, because the world lies in ignorance of God's love and because the Church has failed so miserably in its mission. "My brothers, from the bottom of my heart I long and pray to God that Israel [the world!] may be saved."[16]

A Christian cannot avoid suffering. But perhaps this admission will cause some to turn and ask whether Christ is still worth following in spite of the Church's many errors. Perhaps others will be persuaded that all which is decent and right and good and gospel does indeed outweigh all that is wrong with the Church. And perhaps we Christians will begin to face our failures, honestly awakening to our needs, and willingly accepting our tasks with joy. And all the while we will live hopefully with the promise, "Not by might, not by power, but by my Spirit, saith the Lord."[17]

"Hear, you who have ears to hear,
What the Spirit says to the churches!"[18]

NOTES:

1. James S. Stewart, *A Faith to Proclaim* (New York: Charles Scribner's Sons, 1953), pp. 144,146.
2. Matt. 28:18,20.
3. Matt. 5:29,30 (Phillips).
4. Stephen Neill, *Christian Holiness* (New York: Harper & Row, Inc., 1960), p. 113.
5. I John 3:9 (Phillips).
6. I John 1:8,9 (Phillips).
7. Blaise Pascal, *Pensées,* # 536.
8. John 8:36.
9. Dietrich Bonhoeffer, *Life Together* (New York: Harper & Row, Inc., 1954), pp. 21–22.
10. C. S. Lewis, *Letters to Malcolm* (New York: Harcourt, Brace & World, Inc., 1964), p. 113.
11. *Ibid.,* p. 115.
12. I John 3:2 (*New English Bible*).
13. Quoted by E. Stanley Jones.
14. W. E. Sangster, *The Pure in Heart* (New York: Abingdon Press, 1954), p. 236.
15. See Psa. 1:3.
16. Rom. 10:1 (Phillips).
17. Zech. 4:6.
18. Rev. 3:22 (*New English Bible*).